BLACK WOMEN POETS OF HARLEM RENAISSANCE

Emmanuel E. Egar

University Press of America,® Inc.
Lanham · Boulder · New York · Toronto · Oxford

Copyright © 2003 by
University Press of America,® Inc.
4501 Forbes Boulevard
Suite 200
Lanham, Maryland 20706
UPA Acquisitions Department (301) 459-3366

PO Box 317
Oxford
OX2 9RU, UK

All rights reserved
Printed in the United States of America
British Library Cataloging in Publication Information Available

ISBN 0-7618-2617-3 (paperback : alk. ppr.)

∞™ The paper used in this publication meets the minimum
requirements of American National Standard for Information
Sciences—Permanence of Paper for Printed Library Materials,
ANSI Z39.48—1984

Dedication

For Gwendolyn Oyeba Coleman
who inspired me to remember
those frosty voices of silence.

Contents

Preface		vii
Introduction		ix
Chapter 1	Georgia Douglas Johnson	1
Chapter 2	Anne Spencer	21
Chapter 3	Helen Johnson	27
Chapter 4	Gwendolyn Bennett	47
Chapter 5	Angelina Grimke	53
Chapter 6	Zora Neale Hurston: *Their Eyes Were Watching God*: A Deconstruction	63
Chapter 7	To Criticize the Critics of Zora Neale Hurston's: *Their Eyes Were Watching God*	73
Chapter 8	Dialect as Art in *Their Eyes Were Watching God*	87
Epilogue	The Other Voice of Harlem Renaissance: Langston Hughes	99
Bibliography		111
About the Author		113

Preface

The purpose of this text is to provoke a lively academic discussion on the poetry of Black women in Harlem Renaissance. This discussion is vital not only for public enlightenment, but also to validate the poetic achievements of five sturdy Black women who wrote poetry for poetry, full of joy, passion and even *jouissance*—ecstasy. The validation of the poetic achievements of women in this movement should give us a full realization of the corpus of the Black literary achievements of this era.

It is of interest to note that while the men used poetry as war songs from the mountaintop, women were mainly interested in the enunciation of the Black spirit through poetic meditation. So, if women were silent in terms of belligerent political agitation, their silence should not be construed as a lack of knowledge of that current fight. Their silence can only mean a refusal to speak because of the monstrosity of the utterance. And we should know that when thinking of poetry and politics at this time and as far as women poets were concerned, sometimes it is really difficult to try to separate the dancer from the dance.

Introduction

Black Women Poets of Harlem Renaissance—An Appraisal

Most of the writers on the literary achievements of the poets of Harlem Renaissance focus their attention on Langston Hughes, Claude McKay, Countee Cullen and W.E.B. DuBois. The women poets of this movement are either deliberately or inadvertently omitted or ignored. But it is of interest to know that while the men were using poetry as war songs for freedom, the women seemed to be more interested in writing poetry for poetry, full of passion, spirit, soul and emotions that produced what Roland Barthes called *jouissance*—ecstasy. This statement does not mean that women were not interested in the political struggles of the Black race. It simply means that Black women seemed more interested in poetry for poetry than as a war song from the mountaintop. This text is a humble attempt to define Harlem Renaissance and also critically examine the creative, poetic achievements of five sturdy Black women.

As we attempt to listen to the silent voices of these women, we must first try to understand the meanings and implications of Harlem Renaissance. The search for meanings calls for definitions. And here we face some problems. The problems with definitions are that, according to Kenneth Burke in his *A Grammar of Motives*, definitions never seem to get us to the thinly character of the thing. This means the thingness of things. Definitions seem to end up teasing us with metaphors, similes, allegories and even catachresis. But for lack of an option, we shall use definitions to explain Harlem Renaissance. Webster's *Dictionary* defines Renaissance as, re-animation, rebirth, resurgence, resurrection, resuscitation, revivification, risorgimento. All these words point to one thing: an improvement of a situation or object. Renaissance does not only mean improvement however, it also implies progression, history and resurgence. A resurgence also implies an epiphany—some light. Renaissance is not a revolution because it lacks systematic organization and planning. Perhaps this literary movement among Black writers was an evolution in the form of epiphany, some light that was resoundly enormous. An evolutionary epiphany because most of the leaders of this movement had already mastered the art of writing. They were simply waiting for a chance, a fertile moment, an opportunity to unleash their creative talents.

In the same sense, the word rebirth is not a suitable label because the leaders of this movement did not re-invent anything. Instead, they improved on the old form, a (mimesis) of writing in which some used the Black dialect to a great advantage. So this literary movement was not a rebirth or Renaissance as had been claimed. It was simply an evolutionary epiphany (some light) on a movement to which both men and women contributed greatly.

As we struggle to understand the suitability of the word Renaissance as a label for this Black literary movement, we will also attempt an explanation of the emergence of the fortunes of the city of Harlem in the twenties.

The story of the emergence of the fortunes of the city of Harlem, in New York, is clearly explained in the Norton Anthology of African American Literature. Harlem was a city of paradox. This city, within a city, of New York, was created initially to accommodate rich Whites. But the city lost its clientele because of the economic bursts of the twenties. With this burst and a city structurally sophisticated but with cheap, low-cost housing, the migrating Blacks from the South took hold of it. It was a city that lost its economic nerve, but was rescued by the very people excluded, forbidden and not expected to be there! That was how this city became the Black capital of America in the nineteen twenties.

As we have labored, a labor of love, to deal with the nagging implications of labels, naming, for this literary movement of the Black race, we will now attempt an appraisal of the creative achievements of:

1. Georgia Douglas Johnson
2. Anne Spencer
3. Helen Johnson
4. Gwen Bennett
5. Angelina Grimke

Chapter 1

Georgia Douglas Johnson

> I am folding up my little dreams
> within my heart tonight,
> And praying I may soon forget
> the torture of their sight.
> (*My Little Dreams*)

When we embrace the poetry of Georgia Douglas Johnson, we are immediately reminded of William Wordsworth's definition of poetry. Wordsworth, the British Romantic poet, defined poetry as "emotions recollected in tranquility" or "the overflow of powerful emotions." Poetry for Wordsworth meant feelings, emotions, intuition and the passion to enunciate these sensibilities. In his *Preface to the Literary Ballads*, he gives us a graphic anatomy of the fermentation of emotions, their progression, to a final explosion in a poem. Georgia Johnson's poetry like (William Wordsworth's) carries this bustling sense of emotion, menacing in its grip on a reader to produce *Jouissance*—ecstasy. Her poems that produce these emotions, this joy, this *jouissance* like spiraling drops of honey from heaven are: *The Heart of A Woman, My Little Dreams, I Want to Die While You Love Me*, and *Illusions and Youth*.

A reader's encounter with *The Heart of A Woman* produces this menacing sensation not only in the thought process, but in the development of that thought. Every human heart must leap in pain as we watch the frustrations, the doubts, hopes and desires that a woman's heart undergoes. This heart, like a lone bird, weak, frail and desperate, seems to float through life's toils, foils and foibles to that teasing sensation of a home, that is not really a home, but simple echoes. Echoes that would seem to provoke a desire for a home. A desire that remains a teasing echo that may never come to pass.

This heart of a woman wanders like a lone bird and finally crumbles in a stop, at night (a form of self-strangulation) because it enters an alien cage that completely crushes her dreams, hopes, aspirations and even desires. At this point in the poem, a reader is so saturated, so mesmerized by the beauty of her thought, the paradise of words and the menacing desperation of lost dreams, that you are forced to scream: more, more words, please more! And in a line with the lyrical nostalgia, the thrill, comparable only to Lord Tennyson among English poets, Johnson unleashes the feeling that this heart,

> tries to forget it has dreamed stars,
> while it breaks, breaks, breaks on
> the sheltering bars.

In the above piece, the solid structure of thought in those lines, the anatomy of human frustrations, the desperate inevitability of its helplessness, are the most pleasantly haunting feelings that a poem ever inflicts on a reader. It seems as if the very words and their sounds, the thought and sight are interchangeable.

This passionate nostalgia flows gradually like a river's tendril into *My Little Dreams*. In this poem, the poet moans about the torture of lost dreams. But in this narrative of her frustrations, she takes the reader along this trail, so that we feel for her when she feels, we cry for her, when she cries and in the end, the reader and the poet seem to have undergone the same frustrations, the same anxieties, doubts, hopes and even desires. A metamorphosis of pain!

As we move to hear her heart's endearment in *I Want to Die While You Love Me*, we are ready to cry out like the Greek Sybil in *I Yearn to Die*.

> I want to die while you love me
> While yet you hold me fair
> While laughter lies upon my lips
> and lights are in my hair.
>   (*Norton Anthology*, p. 972, v. 1-5)

In these lines, she reveals that she wants to die while love is at its highest blossom, where sexual intimacy should be so beautiful, that the memory would be eternal. And since it is this love that seems to sustain her life, she does not want it to end.

> I want to die while you love
> me, never, never see
> the glory of this perfect day
> grow dim or cease to be.
> (Ibid v. 13-15)

In this piece, the glory of the day, like love should be eternal. And since it is this love that really makes the day glorious, so, this day like love and light, should never cease. This seems to me to be the most passionate sense of endearment ever seen in poetry.

The Poem: *Old Black Men*

Old Black Men seems to be a requiem to lost hope. A hope taunted and destroyed by anxieties, frustrations, hopes and desires:

> They have dreamed as young men dream,
> of glory, love and power.
> They have hoped as youth will hope,
> of life's sun-minted hour.
> They have seen as others saw
> Their bubbles burst in air,
> And they have learned to live
> it down,
> as though they did not care. (v. 1-8)

This is a sad song, a sad requiem of lost hope, for power, for love and any other kind of human hope for progress. The sad thing about this poem is the absence of mitigating circumstances that could stop this haunting sense of despair. That despair is because "they have seen as others saw, their bubbles burst in air." Here is a story of the synthesis of joy and sadness because the ray of hope in a bubble is that something good would come out of it. But the hostile hands of fate without conscience would burst this hope, this bubble! The point of concern in this poem is that easy surrender, because surrender means death. This sense of defeat and the painful acceptance of this defeat in: "And they learned to live it down as though they did not care," is a heart wrenching sound of loss because every race survives because they believe that there is always hope beyond the rainbow, beyond the stormy clouds and that there may be joy lurking behind the dark tunnel, some ray of hope, tantalizing, desperate, but alluring. This sad and depressing sense of lost hope and the surrender to humiliation is typically feminine. This desperate sense of surrender is a direct opposite of how Claude McKay felt under the same circumstances. His fierce and defiant outburst in *If We Must Die* should wake anybody up from slumber:

> *If We Must Die*
> If we must die, let it be like hogs
> hunted and pinned in an inglorious spot.
> While around us bark the mad and hungry dogs.
> Making their mock at our accursed lot.
> If we must die,
> O let us nobly die
> So that our precious blood may not be shed in vain; then even the monsters we defy,
> Shall be constrained to honor us though dead.
> O Kinsmen! We must meet the common foe
> Though far outnumbered let us
> show us brave
> And for their thousand Blows, deal
> one death blow.
> What though before us lies the open
> grave?
> Like men we'll face the murderers
> cowardly pack,
> pressed to the wall, dying, but
> fighting back. (v. 1-8)

McKay's poem is a war cry from a fanatical general to his men to fight to death. It is also an anatomy of hate relayed in a language that dehumanizes the victim and his oppressors. This really means that in this game of racism both white and black people suffer because of the contagious symbioses of punishment. Punishment destroys the oppressor just the same as it does its victims. That is why McKay inadvertently uses a language meant for animals to describe human beings. The Black people are "hogs," while the white people are "murderous mad dogs."

But in his fervent, provocative inspiration to his troops, he could not see the disabling implications of his call. The disturbing implications are what a good military general never misses. Some of these implications are:

1. That, when surrounded and outnumbered, the best defense is a surrender.
2. That, the death of a general weakens the morale of his troops.
3. That in death, there are no heroes.
4. That if everybody dies in a fight, you really have lost. Lost Big!!

It is for this reason that suicide is a stupid crime because it is violence against oneself. This crime may only be enjoyable to the masochist because he/she enjoys seeing himself/herself die in dying. So, while for Georgia Johnson, "Old Black Men" die with their anxieties, frustrations, hopes and desires, for McKay it is better to die fighting so as to keep what hope alive?

However, from the poem of lost hope, we move to the futility of all forms of discrimination between white/black, between rich and poor as if all these human cravings can bring us eternal life. The poem *Common Dust* should remind us of John Donne's poem *Death Be Not Proud*. Donne's contention was that if he has achieved all he ever wanted out of life, then death has nothing to gain. Death has not deprived him anything. So, death should not be proud. But Donne, like all teachers of morality, they teach like angels, but live like men. Even when Donne was throwing all those tirades at death, it was also the time he was most afraid of death. His tirades really appear as an apology to death!

In Georgia Johnson's *Common Dust*, death is an equalizer between white/black, poor/rich and Jew/Gentile. The poet claims that if we only know the commonality and inevitability of death to all human beings, then discrimination of any kind would simply be ranting stupidity.

Common Dust
And who shall separate the dust,
which later we shall be: whose
keen discerning eyes will scan,
and solve the mystery?
The high, the low, the rich, the
poor, the black, the white . . .

> And whom shall it be said:
> Here lies the dust of Africa.
> Here are the sons of Rome.
> Here lies one unlabeled.
> The world at large his home!
> Can one then separate,
> will mankind lie apart,
> when life has settled back again?
> The same as from start. (v. 1-10)

In this poem, Johnson is concerned with a common human scourge. That scourge of discrimination! Discrimination between nations, between rich and poor, between white people and black. Her contention is, if we only knew that we all have one common destiny: "Death," then all our common antagonism would disappear because of its very futility. The poem seems to gain intensity from the rhetorical question:

> Who shall separate the dust
> and solve the mystery!

The beauty of a rhetorical question is that the question itself may be the answer, just as the answer is that question. And all this is because the poet does not seriously require an answer to her question. So, because of the open ended nature of this question, it provokes endless significations that go on "ad infinitum." But Johnson deflates this intensity when she provides answers to this rhetorical question at the last stanza of the poem. This means that the aura, that sense of mystery is then bursted and it dissipates into air! We see her answers in:

> Can one then separate the dust,
> will mankind lie apart,
> when life has settled back again.
> The same as from the start!

Here, the poet deflates the intensity, that sense of mystery, associated with rhetorical questions by supplying answers to a serious riddle that turns out to be really juvenile. The answers are that nobody can separate the dust from dust of mankind because of that scourge, that eternal maxim,

"Dust thou art, dust thou shall
return." We are all one in death.

This poem about death leads us to the poem: *Escape*.

This poem: *Escape* because it comes immediately after *Common Dust* of death, seems to bear the same aura or contentions of death. This sense of sadness, of sorrow seems to flow in from the common destiny of man: Death. But the poem's narrative logic does not bear out this trend of thought if we interrogate it with a question like: Whose shadow is the poet craving, calling on to protect her from sorrow? There may be several explanations for this shadow. One is that the shadow may be the shadow of death, of suffering, of repression or many other social problems of the day. Maybe it is the shadow of death and decay that frightens the poet. Maybe it is the shadow of the helplessness of her race in the face of human humiliations. Maybe in the intensity of these social problems, sometimes, man craves an escape into himself/herself, into their shadow, into the wind or even thin air. But every attempt to escape from sorrow without solving the source or cause of that sorrow is usually futile. That is why:

By sorrow:
She pursues me everywhere
I can't lose her anywhere.

The critical contention in this poem, however, is in the misty, murky thought process which opens doors to speculations like: "Who is it that pursues me everywhere," and "I can't lose her." Is this the shadow or the sorrow? Or could it be that in the heated anxieties of social problems in the poet's mind, the words (sorrow/shadow) are synthesized, a form of mutation, an alchemy where these two words lose their individual or collective meaning (a form of neutrality) to produce only one eternal symbol of: Helplessness? The confusion in this part of the poem stems from the fact that from the narrative logic of this poem, the word "shadow" and "sorrow" are interchangeable. This seems to be a case of confusion in thought by the poet!

However, since the poet is bent on escaping her sorrow, she craves the shadows to:

Fold me in your black abyss.

Here again, we run smack into a confusion in the thought process to a point that we are forced to ask the question: who is (she/it/he) "who will never look in this." Is it sorrow that will not penetrate itself? All these questions and speculations do not make any logical sense. And so, these unanswered questions point only one way: confused thought process. The overriding contention, however, is that because of some unknown experiences, the poet craves an escape, a refuge, a sanctuary into some shadows. Shadows that serve as a sanctuary and insulation from pain. But even here we run into another obstacle which is: If her whole idea is to escape from sorrow, why does she want the shadows to: "Hug me round in your solitude." The question here is: Does solitude, seclusion, neutralize sorrow? In fact, does solitude, seclusion not intensify sorrow because of the scourge of loneliness and alienation? Sadly, however, from the poetry of Johnson, we will never know because of the self castigating syllogism of: Poetic License.

The poems of Georgia Douglas Johnson, that we have discussed so far, touch on the themes of death, human destiny, escape into shadows, all of which tend to evoke a sad despairing tone. The poem: *Suppliant* has a familiar tone of sadness. But this is a sadness with a different twist. However, before we discuss the narrative logic and conclusion of the poem, let us try to understand the etymological and semantic nuances of *Suppliant*. The word provokes some rather curious significations because it tends to imply submission, subservience, servile, supplication, earnest entreaty, humility, beseeching, a beggarly conduct by one on the lower scale of the social spectrum. The narrative thrust of the poem is that despite the poet's humble and servile prayers to God, her prayers were not rewarded—a fate quite similar to that of her ancestors. But despite these failures, these anxieties, these doubts, frustrations, hopes and desires, the poet has the wisdom to counsel: "The strong demand, contend, prevail, the beggar is a fool."

The wisdom of that counsel has obvious insinuations worthy of exploration. The central point is that the notion of humility even to God is just as unprofitable as the fool who begs. Supplication to God or man is not profitable because in certain instances the only action that seems to bring quick results is a show of strength, of contending, which leads to progress. So, through the title of the poem, the narrative logic seems to be dancing to the tunes of different drummers, yet the conclusion of the poem enunciates the wisdom in political education. An education that unleashes a truism that: the strong demand, contend, prevail; the beggar is a fool.

The other side of this argument is that because you use your strength to negotiate with demands does not mean your demands will be met. The fact also is that because you contend does not mean that you will always prevail. And sometimes if we listen to biblical wisdom, we lose to win and even win to lose. Also, the beggar may not always be the fool. Sometimes in the trials of life, we need the resources of the beggar and the fool to win. This poem reveals the height of political frustration when even God will not respond to prayers and man is forced to take matters into his own hands. But when we do this, when we decide to play God, we falter because unlike God, we are incapable of seeing all the corners of an event. These frustrations from a God who is silent, when compounded with human repressions, strictures on individual and communal progress, may seem to build a momentum for violence. This need for violence is relayed in the poem *Prejudice*.

The poem *Prejudice* spreads like a universal miasma, inflicting its strictures and repressions on all forms of progress because it "tightens my little world around," "stills the soaring will to wing" and stops the "dance" and stagnates progress. But despite all the humiliation, man is not bowed. That is why:

> beneath incrusted silences,
> a seething Etna lies,
> the fire of whose furnace may sleep
> But never dies.

The thrust of the poem is that no amount of humiliation can ever kill a determined human spirit. Repression, instead, creates anger and a hunger to revenge in order to win. And victory is usually won by those who persevere! Johnson's trail of resistance to racism and repression trickles through most of the poems in this selection from the lost hope and dreams of (*Old Black Men*); the common destiny in death in *Common Dust*; the sorrows that drive man to his own shadows in *Escape*; the poignant tragedy of a God who is silent in the midst of human suffering *The Suppliant*; and the degrading, stifling strictures in *Prejudice*. The message is the same! That message is that in the face of painful humiliation, the Black race must dig into their deepest human and psychical reserve for strength, so as to command, contend, prevail. To surrender is to be like the fool who is a beggar with lost hopes.

All these poems serve as strings of political education for the black race. And as if the education of the victim and the victimizer is not complete, Johnson unleashes a warm and beautiful sermon like Jesus Christ in his Beatitudes, in *The Sermon on the Mount*. Just as in the Beatitudes, Christ laid down the foundation of peace and morality for mankind, Johnson enunciates a universal credo, a belief, a truism that should educate and yet even sustain not only the victim, but also the victimizer in the poem *Prejudice*.

The poem *Prejudice* opens with:

I believe in the ultimate justice of
fate:
That the races of men front the sun
in their turn;
That each soul holds the title to
infinite wealth.
In fee to the will as it masters
itself.
That the heart of humanity sounds
the same tone.
In impious jungle or sky-kneeling
fane.
I believe that the key to life
mystery
Lies deeper than reason and
further than death.
I believe that the rhythmical
conscience within
Is guidance enough for the conduct
of men. (v. 1-9)

This poem has these sobering prescriptions that could improve the quality of social interaction for all mankind if only we believe and act on it. And there are some beautiful insinuations to the content of the credo for several reasons. First, if you believe in the ultimate justice of fate, you will also believe that God's time is the best. But since this time has no design, no plan, no date, if you wait for fate to settle your scores, you will wait indefinitely. That is why those who strive, struggle, usually succeed. Those who wait on fate do not because that mythical wheel of fortune has no conscience, no friends, and no enemies. Secondly, if you believe that the human race "front the sun in their own turn," you will also believe in man's common destiny, in death, judgement and eternity. If you believe in all these, you will make every moment in life count. You will also believe in the universal philosophy of fairness and in that great maxim: Live and let Live! Similarly, if you believe that:

> Each soul holds the title to infinite wealth,
> In fee to the will as it masters itself.

You proclaim the wisdom of the goodness of each human being, and so validate the propensity of each human will to act right. But these are vaunting ideals. These are like building sky scrappers in the air. These are illusions because man has the greatest capacity within context for good and evil. The reverse side of this point is that it is because man has deliberately not used his will to engage the natural human goodness that we have all the multifarious problems of race and discrimination. The contention that "the heart of humanity sounds the same tone, in impious jungle or sky-kneeling fane," is a universal statement that suffers from all other attributes of universalism. A universal statement because it is always stereotypical, represses dissident voices and so imposes the master/servant syndrome. But in the context of this poem, it may be safe to say that all human hearts do not respond identically to bad or joyful situations. Man is varied in his motives and bewitching in his/her capacity for manipulation. That is why people respond to any situation individually or collectively due to their individual anxieties, frustrations, doubts, hopes and desires. The notion of a universal human consciousness that is basically good is a flagrant over exaggeration of an idealism. Also the truism that: the key to life's mystery lies deeper than reason and further than death, can be accepted, except that it raises other questions about the meaning of reason and death. Reason, we can speculate on from Socrates (man know thyself) Descartes (Cogito ego Sum) Liebniz (Nihil est sine ratione) and even Milan Kundera in his: Man thinks, God laughs! But death! What do we know about death? A monster that comes to you like a thief in the night when you are least prepared. The only way we could know anything about death is to die and watch ourselves dying. But this is a buried memory!

There is however, a common acceptance that "the rhythmic conscience within is guidance enough for the conduct of men." This is a purist and puritanical assumption that the good Lord has planted his ten commandments in every human heart. This assumption has compounding and complicating implications. The first problem for this universal conscience is the vagaries surrounding the word "conscience" and its link with the *Ten Commandments*. And since commandments have a link with Christianity, this leaves the non-Christians, the atheists without conscience. Commandments also have a link with morality and ethics. We know also that morals and ethics have subjective and communal implications. So, all these fragile links would make sense if every human being believed in the God of Moses and Abraham! But the world is not so evenly gifted with conscience, since not all people in the world believe in God. So, if the Christians act according to conscience, what about the non-Christians, the unbelievers? Do they have a conscience? If not, how do they conduct their human behaviors. This notion of universal conscience has too many complexities/complications, dennotations/connotations and significations that could go on "ad infinitum." In conclusion, we can safely say that conscience and human conduct are beautiful but questionable ideals.

There is a common axiom, a universal dictum which says that the best teachers are those who teach with: motivation, empathy and reinforcement. Georgia Douglas Johnson's next set of poems embrace these themes. Some of the poems in this consideration include: *Trifle, The Poet Speaks, Your World and Conquest*.

The poem *Trifle* celebrates the joy in the efficacy of humor, the comic that aims at oneself, the comic relief. This comic, this self depreciating humor should be stored away (as it were) in a sanctuary so that we could visit it in bad times for relief and inspiration:

> Against the day of sorrow
> lay by some trifling thing
> A smile, a kiss, a flower
> for sweet remembering
> Then when the day is darkest
> without one rift of blue
> take out four little trifle
> and dream your dream anew. (p. 21, v. 1-8)

The beauty of the above poem is in that systematic and well developed thought process where the meaning, the syntax and even words reinforce the themes of motivation, empathy and reinforcement. The advice to store away little joys, jokes, kisses, bliss and pleasure so that we could go back for them in bad times, offers not only comic relief, but a solace in hard times. And perhaps, the most beautiful energy that they unleash on this victim of sadness and boredom, is that he/she not only strives but actually dreams his/her way to success. It is quite important that every human being should have these little trifles, joys stored away in one emotional and psychological sanctuary for use when needed. The language and the vocabularies in this poem are beautiful because of their nuances, insinuations that instigate reverberations, vibrations—teasing significations that have a domino effect. For instance, to use the word "lay" to signify putting away trifles, immediately evokes that metaphor of the symbolic and the concrete, synonymous to laying down brick walls to start a building. The word "lay" as it appears in the context has an ingenious implication which hovers over the metaphysical conceit of John Donne. It is a semantic implication in which a word craves a meaning as well as mocking this very meaning of its craving. And the word "rift" as used in the poem to separate darkness from darkness has the same implications of metaphysical conceit because the rift implies a mild or violent dramatic break (a kind of mirror dance) where the negative and positive elements separate (commenting and negating each other) in that conscious neutrality. Georgia Douglas Johnson has this powerful and native syllogism that has a quintessential embrace of poetic license! The poem, *The Poet Speaks*, embraces the same themes of motivation, empathy and reinforcement.

In this poem: *The Poet Speaks*, Johnson assumes the role of a seer, a prophet like (Isaiah and Jeremiah) who advise, counsel, praise and admonish the children of Israel for spiritual sanctification (a moral cleansing) aimed at making them acceptable vessels in the eyes of Jehovah. And in Jeremiah's eyes the children of Israel should strive to be an (ecclesia pura) a visible community of saints from the midst of which the black sheep must be taken away so that it does not offend the eyes of God. The poem: *The Poet Speaks*, opens with a repetition of a highly coded and condensed question:

> How much living have you done?
> From it the patterns that you weave
> are imaged:
> Your own life is your totem pole,
> your yard of cloth,
> your living.
> How much living have you done?
> How full and free your giving?

For living is but loving
and loving only giving. (p. 22, v. 1-10)

The above poem gives me a feeling that the poet's religious (bible school teaching) is beginning to creep into her poetry. This religious insinuation can be seen from the theme of loving and giving (cardinal doctrines of Christianity) that seem to permeate the two verses above. So, the question, "How much living have you done?" is not an enquiry about the age of the individual. Instead, it demands the content, quantity and quality of this content and quantity of life. The native and traditional implication of the phrase: "How much" immediately provokes a monetary and economic implication of value and expenditure. But the poet is not really concerned with the market economics of price, value and expenditure. So, by means of semantic transfer, the question "how much" becomes a muted metaphor, a catachresis of the quality of the value and expenditure of life! The question demands an account of how one has lived; how he/she has dealt with the frustrations, anxieties, mutilations, doubts, hopes and even desires of life. It is the pattern of dealing with these problems and symptoms of life that determines ones image. That is why one's life becomes not only a symbolic image, but a concrete sign pole and yard stick for the measurement of the quality of human life. This poetic role of a poet as a seer, a prophet who encourages as well as admonishes his followers is relayed again in the poem, *Your world*:

Your world is as big as you make it.
I know, for I used to abide
In the narrowest nest in a corner,
My wings pressing close to my side.
But I sighted the distant horizon
where the sky line encircled the sea
and I throbbed with a burning
desire
to travel this immensity.
I battered the cordons around me
and cradled my wings on the
breeze
then soared to the uttermost
reaches
with rapture, with power,
with ease! (p. 23, v. 1-12)

The tone, thrust, meaning and semantic enunciations of this poem begin to sound like a motivational speech given to high school graduating seniors. Our concern here is the matter of humility and modesty. Our concern here is that since the office of the poet from its traditional inception was supposed to be a seer, a mouthpiece and voice of Jehovah, God, Himself, can a poet claim to be successful? Since she is only the messenger? By claiming to be successful, has she taken the place of God? Or has she synthesized the role of the messenger with that of the master and yet serving both collectively and individually, successfully? The poet, I thought, was to be humble because she/he depends and listens to the master's voice! We can take a nostalgic journey back into history, even to Saint Augustine, to witness the modesty and humility of the poet. Not even the youngest and brightest of English poets, John Keats, could claim success; that he had arrived? In fact, Keats moaned that he is only sure to be famous after his death! Shakespeare may have seen himself in Othello:

> the Savage Indian who
> threw away a pearl
> richer than all his tribe.

T.S. Eliot may have seen his pathetic dejection in *Pruffrock* when he agonized in:

> I will wear white flannel
> Trousers, and walk along
> the beach.
> I hear the mermaids
> Singing each to each
> I do not think they will
> Sing to me.

There is a sound of sadness, of self depreciating pathos in both Shakespeare and Eliot; both of a different kind. In Shakespeare's *Othello*, it is the ignorant stupidity of the noble savage that echoes. In Eliot it is a humility tempered by self pity at his lack of success even in his successes. This arrogance of self praise perhaps surfaces only in Samuel Johnson's *Rasellas,* where the poet Imlac, claims that the poet should be the legislator of all mankind. But even here, the poet does not claim individual artistic or social success because the real success of the legislator (the Seer) comes from the master, the man who sent him, God Himself. Now that we have dealt with a writer's personal bias (Eliot) or the rooted political concern (Accocella's) we can now subject the poem to a literary appreciation wondering: Does the poem succeed as a literary work of art? Or does excessive individualism, the claims of artistic, social and political success destroy the poem? These are not easy questions because poetic judgement is usually subjective. However, we will judge this poem based on: The anatomy of the thought process, the use of words and their significations, the development of the thought processes, the compelling philosophic vision, and the suitability of this vision to the context.

The central idea of the poem is that success is an individual thing. That, if you are hungry enough to succeed, you will work, do whatever it takes, to succeed. But how is this thought developed? The poet opens her inspirational speech with a universal statement:

> Your world is as big as you make it.

The implication here is that if you think big, dream big, you will get there. But universal statements have problems because since they are always stereotypical, they often neglect individual cases. A universal statement also seems to suppress individual voices and so, usually proclaims the master and servant syndrome. And as if anticipating the negations of this syndrome, the poet points out her individual success and what it took to be successful. This thought of individual success is dressed up so beautifully with words which tell a story as if in simulation, so that the words, sounds and meaning, seem to be interchangeable. The thought of the poet hiding as a sparrow in "The narrowest nest in a corner, my wings pressing close to my side," evokes such sense of dread, of fear, of agonizing deprivation particularly when seen through that exclusive seclusion of a nest. A nest which sets boundaries, restrictions, control—all of which are calculated to whittle ambition and even progress. The poet then proceeds to enunciate the anatomy of her efforts, her anxieties, frustrations, hopes and desires in:

> But I sighted the distant horizon
> Where the sky line encircled the sea.
> And I throbbed with a burning desire,
> To travel this immensity. (v. 4-8)

The above is a story of hope in "distant horizon" dreams and determination in "I throbbed with a burning desire" that show a curiosity and desire to succeed. Lurking in this verse is the underlined sense of vision and a haunting hope to achieve that vision. The poet then unleashes the anatomy of her determination to overcome her frustrations, mutilations, doubts, hopes and even desire that pushed her beyond the threshold to success. Her efforts and determination are relayed in words like: "battered," "cordons," all of which have condensed dennotations/connotations, complicity/complications that have far reaching significations. The word "battered" has elusive significations.

It could mean a trade (off) of one thing for another. It could also mean defeating a group in a fight. But in the context of the poem that embraces the word "cordons" (a line of men or ships stationed to guard or enclose an area) the poet implies a forceful effort to break the barriers that seemed to restrict and control her progress. There is in this poem a beautiful wedding between an idea, a meaning and the words used to communicate that idea and meaning. This means that there is really an amazing synthesis between personal bias, the social and political, to produce a very successful poem. The next scrutiny of the poem is whether the philosophic vision and context make any intellectual sense!

The philosophic vision of: "You can succeed if you struggle hard enough," when coupled with examples of success using the same methods can produce amazing results to a down trodden people. This is a motivation that can pull people out of welfare, attract youths to school and persuade them to stay in and graduate. In Georgia Johnson, we see this joyful interplay of meaning and language, diction, syntax and simulation, so that it should remind the reader of Roland Barthes's *Pleasure of Performance of a Text*:

> The feat is to sustain the mimesis of Language (language
> imitating itself) The source of immense pleasures, in a
> Fashion so fadically ambiguous (ambiguous to the root)
> That the text never succumbs to the good conscience
> (And bad faith) of parody (of castrating laughter of the
> Comical that makes us laugh. (p. 9)

The pleasure of performance of language in Georgia Johnson's poetry performs a feat that sustains the mimesis of language (language imitating and even mocking) itself as we see in her use of metaphysical conceit. We see in Johnson, a poetic language so radically ambiguous that it never succumbs to good conscience particularly when that poetic language is used in the service of political motivation. We see in Johnson's poetic language, a language of parody, "of castrating laughter of the comical that makes us laugh" particularly when we see her lack of modesty or humility in claiming economic, social and even poetic success. A success that a poet as a seer reserves only for the supreme deity. But if the poet in: "Your world" was inspired to motivate her people through individual examples, of what it takes to tame our anxieties, mutilations, frustrations, doubts, hopes and desires to succeed; the poet of: "Conquest," is traumatized and stifled by the same anxieties, frustrations, doubts, hopes and the same desires:

The Poem: *Conquest*, opens with:

My path lies through worse than death;
I meet the hours with bated breath.
My red blood boils, my pulses thrill,
I live life running up a hill.
Ah, no, I need no paltry play
Of make shift tilts for holiday:
For I was born against the tide
and I must conquer that denied.
I shun no hardship, fear no foe;
The future calls and I must go.
I charge the line and dare the spheres
As I go fighting down the years. (v. 1-2)

In the first stanza of this poem, *Conquest*, the poet is traumatized by problems that provoke her anxieties, doubts and desires. It is because of this trauma that her path is worse than death. That is why her "breath" is "bated," her "blood boils" and even her "pulse thrills" like she is about to have a cardiac arrest. Her problems are so stupendous that it looks like she is running up a hill in an attempt to solve these problems. But, beaten, tormented, the poet is not bowed. The poet relays her problems with dignity that is devoid of self-pity. She knows she can not enjoy the luxury of a vacation because she was born against the tide. But despite all these problems, these frustrations, these doubts, she must achieve success that seemed denied her because of the accident of birth. Her struggles continue.

So, in the next stanza (third) despite all her problems, it seems that she becomes stronger. That is why she "shuns no hardship" and "fears no foe" and so she must throw herself recklessly into the future; take a chance whenever opportunities appear in the future. It will seem as if the more problems she meets, the stronger she becomes. That is why, like a mad officer in the army, she has "charged the line, dared the spheres" and went down fighting like a good soldier. This poem should remind the reader of Shakespeare's charge on how to be successful in his:

> There is a tide in the affairs
> of men,
> which when taken at the flood
> leads on to fortune.
> But if left, all the
> sails are lost in shallows
> and miseries." (Julius Caesar)

I wonder who said: Nobody wins success who does not strive?

Chapter 2

Anne Spencer

> No woman in all Persia sets out
> strange action
> To confuse Persia's Lord—
> Love is but desire and thy
> purpose fulfillment;
> I, thy King say so!
>   (*Before The Feast of Shushan*)

Anne Spencer is a poet of mixed anxieties on gender problems. These gender anxieties stem from her doubts about the efficacy of the marriage institution (*Feast of Shushan*) the tensions and contentions on Lesbianism (*Carnival*; *Lady, Lady*; *A Letter to My Sister*) the burden of womanhood (wife-woman) and man's helplessness in a cosmos beyond our control in *Dunbar*.

Spencer's anxieties on the efficacy of the marriage institution are carefully relayed in her poem: *Before the Feast of Shushan*. Here is a poem whose whole purpose seems to be the dramatization of the power game in sexual relationship between the King and Queen.

This game is staged under a beautiful setting, the evocation of a beautiful scene like heaven and paradise, with the beautiful splendor of the Queen, magnificent and charming, are vividly captured. In this poem, love is a sacrament which is reminiscent of a sacrifice by a willing Christ on the cross for our sins. But for Christ, the sacrament and sacrifice were voluntary, while the love relationship between the King and Queen is not. This is because the omniscient King must be obeyed when he demands sexual intimacy. But in the poem, the Queen seems to stage a resistance, thereby questioning the rationale and even foundation of this sexual game where the male King is so domineering while the Queen is supposed to be submissive and even passive! This insinuation of sexual resistance begins to sound like a feminist insurrection aimed at demanding respect, dignity and the humane treatment of women not only when dealing with sex, but in all aspects of human life. The King's egotistical arrogance comes out in these lines:

> I, thy Lord, like not manna for
> meat as a Judahn.
> I, thy Master, drink red wine
> plenty and when I thirst.
> Eat meat, and full when I hunger
> I, thy King, teach you and leave
> when I list.
> No woman in all Persia sets out
> action,
> To confuse Persia's Lord.
> Love is but desire and thy
> purpose fulfillment;
> I, thy King, so say.
>   (*Norton Anthology*, p. 947, v. 38-40)

Here is the display of the arrogant, monarchial power, where the King gets what he wants and when he wants it. He is not desperately dependent on God like the children of Israel who depended on God to feed them with manna from heaven in the desert. For this King and the tradition of his lineage, love is desire and the Queen's purpose is to satisfy that desire without questioning. It is this trend of thought that ignites all kinds of vibrations because for the modern world, love is a willing, voluntary, mutual relationship of sharing. This poem may be a hint, a questioning of the prevailing sexual mores of the time. And in questioning, the poet hoped to educate the world and to change the disturbing sexual plights of women. As Paul Jean Sartre taught us so warmly, the purpose of literature is to expose the glaring anomalies of society so as to change them. And like an afterthought, calculated to deflect the reader's mind from the theatre of the poet's mind, the poet unleashes a requiem to the poem: *Dunbar*.

    The poem, *Dunbar* is a lament on the helplessness of man in a world beyond his control. It is for this helplessness that all poets, despite their life sustaining poems, yet still die. The poet then takes a nostalgic journey into history to mourn the great English poets like: John Keats, Shelley and Charterton. And here, Spencer provokes a rival, my second coming into the study of great English poets, wondering what is it, that led a poet, to poets so as to feed on nostalgia. A desperate craving and yearning!

The poem, *Dunbar*, was a real smoke-screen to the main theatre of the poet's mind. The theatre of Spencer's mind seems to be at how man's egocentricity, as symbolized by the King's arrogance, seems to drive women to Lesbianism, as a sanctuary for feminine peace and comfort. These Lesbian insinuations are first revealed in a poem called: *At the Carnival*.

The poem: *At the Carnival*, immediately begins to insinuate Gay/Lesbian cravings as we see the poet, the Limousine Lady and the Male Driver vying for the same girl in *Carnival* trunks. The poet then pours disturbing praises on this beautiful girl. She refers to her as "the gleaming girl," the "leaven of the earth," and even "God." This is a baffling sense of woman to woman infatuation. But the sad thing is that because of societal pressures and sanctions, her infatuation must remain silent and so, she calls on the god Neptune to rescue her from her craving and the unsatisfied sexual quest.

It may be logical to speculate that when we watch the arrogant dominance of monarchial power in *Shushan* garden the poet's sympathy seems to shift naturally to protecting women by providing them sanctuary for sexual freedom. Spencer's obsessions with Lesbianism filter through poems like: *Lady, Lady*; and *A Letter to My Sister*.

In *Lady, Lady*, her feminine gaze focuses on the beautiful black lady who is as "dark as night withholding a star." But this gaze soon moves from the skin to the heart of this woman, where "there is a dark-some place were tongues of flames the ancients knew" and where "the god sits to spangled through," all of which seem to reveal sexual insinuations of woman to woman, from a woman with repressed sexual passions for a fellow woman. These Lesbian obsessions surface again in: *A Letter to My Sister*.

In this poem, she seems to struggle with herself to express what seems inexplicable. A reader can almost feel her frustrations as she taunts herself in:

> It is dangerous for a woman to
> defy the gods

To taunt them with the tongues thin
lips
Or straut in the weakness of
mere humanity.
> (*Norton Anthology*, p. 949, v. 1-5)

This section of the poem provokes a critical question. And that question is: What is it that God designed a woman to do, that if she fails to do it, she would be defying the command of God?! The answer here may be a theological one. The theological answer is that God made a woman to be a mate to a man. She would be defying God's command if instead of man, a woman picked another woman for a mate! The unspoken hint here is that since marriage between a man and woman always seems to be battle grounds for female abuse and disagreement, a woman maybe safer with another woman. This is feminism at its best, but it also leads to the demise of the human race because a woman needs a man for procreation and human continuity. However, Spencer's anxieties with gender issues do not end only in Lesbianism. It melts into womanhood and the tedium, the sheer burden of motherhood.

We engage this motherhood anxiety in: *The Wife-Woman*. Here, the title of the poem stages a textural tension, a kind of preamble with rhetorical insinuations like: What does it mean to be a woman and a wife?! Are you a wife first and a woman second or vice versa? Can a woman synthesize the two into a beautiful blend or can both co-exist in their individualities, and still serve the marriage institution? Put differently, can one separate the woman from the wife or the wife from the woman without damage to both? This reasoning should recall the Yeatsian Romantic image of the Dancer and the Dance. However, this preamble, this text before the text, maybe fully understood when we confront the poem.

This poem opens with an invocation of the resilience of a mother with seven children whose spirit the poet compares to that of the mariner who confronts a storm, unshaken even with its biting turbulence. But, then, almost as an afterthought, or the explosion from a suppressed anger, the protagonist or the poet lashes out:

I can not love them;
And I feel your glad chiding from
the grave,

> That my all was only worth at all
> What joy to you it gave
> These seven links the law
> compelled from human chain—
> I can not love them; and you,
> Oh, seven-fold months in Flanders
> Slain.
>   (*Norton Anthology*, p. 950, v. 10-16)

This statement, "I can not love them," really is a negation of affirmation because how can she not love the children that bring joy to her dead mother from the grave? How can she not love the children born to fulfill God's command to a woman "to increase and multiply"? But realistically, she can not love them (take care of seven children) alone and still retain her sanity and womanhood! And the statement is haunting and disturbing because it provokes all kinds of insinuations from its built-in vague completion that may itself provoke questions like: I can not love them . . . because? Because of what? This silence is as disturbing as it is haunting because it does not mean the inability to speak. It means a refusal to speak the unspeakable because of the monstrosity around its utterance. Maybe she can not love them because of the sheer tedium of the human burden of raising seven children alone. She can not love them, perhaps, because she does not really want to be a wife. She can not separate the woman from the wife while staying faithful to both.

However, as paradoxical as this point seems, there are also two conflicting currents running through the poem. One is the biblical imperative to have more children. A view that is validated by the dead mother from her grave. Then comes this abrasive resistance from a woman who is burdened and frustrated from having too many children in: *I Can Not Love Them*. A deliberate and determined rejection of what one is supposed to love. A negation of affirmation!

Chapter 3

Helen Johnson

Gee, Brown Boy, I Loves You All Over;
I'm Glad I'm a Jig;
Poem

If Georgia Johnson has the passionate romantic flavors of William Wordsworth, Anne Spencer has the gender anxieties leaning towards obsession with Lesbianism. This really means that both poets had deliberate themes through which they decided to enunciate their anxieties. But what about the other women who were not obedient to themes? Those who wrote poetry for poetry, full of joy, passion and soul that were completely oblivious to thematic implications! Those whose topics were as varied and scattered as feathers in a bustling summer storm! Poets like, Helen Johnson, Gwendolyn Bennett and Angelina Grimke, fall into this joyful category.

Helen Johnson's poetry touches on the love of Jazz music, Negro pride, culture and love. Some of her poems that deal with these topics include: *Poem* (Negro Jazz); *Sonnet to a Negro in Harlem* (Negro pride/culture); *Remember Not* (Love); *Invocation* (Love).

The piece: *Poem* is a joyful evocation of the passionate love for Jazz music and the Negro excitement with it. In this poem, the poet touches on universal Negro beauty, the Negro enchantment with Jazz and the thrill of the Jazz movement. The intensity of her feeling seems to accelerate into sexual passion when she engages the Black dialect:

> Gee, Boy, I loves you all over.
> I am glad I'm a jig. I'm glad

> I can understand your dancing
> and your singing, and feel all
> the happiness,
> And joy and don't care in you.
>   (*Norton Anthology*, p. 1316, v. 14-18)

There is an intimacy of feeling in, "I loves you all over." There is also a communal closeness and attachment not only to the musician, but the music because she almost instinctively enjoys the music even with her ears closed. There is also this flirtation between sexual infatuation and the genuine love for Jazz music. But the poet controls this flow of emotions so that she may concentrate on the poem, the thought process and the progression of that thought. She seems to control these emotions, letting them filter like beautiful rain tendrils throughout the body of the poem. But this passionate movement of thought is suddenly invaded by the intrusion of an alien word—"Tomtoms" into the poem. This surprised intrusion raises some local, communal questions which seem also to have sublime universal appeal. And the following lines have their own story:

> Listen to me, will you,
> What do I know about tomtoms?
> But, I like the word,
> Sort of, don't you?
> It belongs to us.
>   (Ibid v. 22-25)

This command, quick and abrasive, may be directed at some individuals or the universal Negro consciousness about Jazz. And the rhetorical question, "What do I know about Jazz?" playful, gentle and yet poignantly effective because she provokes a thought process like a (domino) that seems to unleash another thought process. The answer to this rhetorical question may be in the question and the question itself may be the answer. The question itself has a labyrinth of implications bordering on the Negro's attachment to Africa. This African insinuation stems from the fact that "tomtoms" and "balofung" are musical instruments used in Senegal, a small country in West Africa. Leopold Senghor made the "tomtom" and "balofung" famous in his Negritude poetry. So, the Negro can rightly claim ownership of the word particularly if she claims Africa as her ancestral home! The poem really is a beautiful evocation of the thrills of Jazz music. A beauty that is intensified by the strong feelings for Jazz as well as the sexual flirtations of the lyric.

However, if *Poem* deals with Negro excitement with Jazz, the poem, *Sonnet to a Negro in Harlem*, demonstrates the theme of the Noble savage who is strong, barbaric and defiant of his oppressors. There is a temptation to feel that the gesture of thought in the poem is towards the affirmation of the strong inner and physical strength of the Negro. But the poet ruins this affirmation with too many negative insinuations about the Negro's incapacities. To describe the Negro with words like: disdainful, pompous, incompetent, barbaric and supercilious brings out too much of negative flavors to a point that they easily crush any other positives left standing in the poem. And I do not think that the theme of the noble savage is suitable for the enunciation of the Negritude feelings in this poem. The term, the "Noble Savage" itself, shows the nagging inadequacies in the internal content and craving of English language. A language so inadequate that it seems to mock a feeling, a meaning, a thought that it finds inexplicable. It really sounds horrifying to try to love what one really hates. That would be the death of language! Helen Johnson is a poet who takes pride in Negro culture and Negro pride. But it is also a job that she does poorly because of the excessive infusion of negations in describing Negro qualities. However, I think that she does a better job in her discussions of love and self pity and also the self sustaining power of true human love.

The demonstration of love and self pity are relayed in her poem called: *Remember Not*. The poem, *Remember Not,* sounds like a requiem of self pity from a woman who feels that age alone may have tarnished her beauty and the corresponding affection from her lover:

> You must not through mistaken
> chivalry, pretend to love me still.
>   (*Norton Anthology*, p. 1317, v. 10-11)

At this point in the poem, the reader is caught in a bout of conflicting tensions and contentions as to what really is believable: To believe or not to believe her pleas! And so, several questions immediately surge into the mind like: Is true love, purely physical? What about spiritual and mental love? Is true love merely seasonal? There is an inclination for a reader to rove into metaphysical poetic conceit in search of meaning for these pleas. But the central feeling in the poem seems really to be directed towards self pity for getting old. This kind of feeling should immediately remind the reader of the pathetic moanings of T.S. Eliot's *J. Alfred Prufrock* in:

> I grow old. I grow old.
> I have measured out my life
> with coffee spoons . . .
> I hear the mermaids singing each
> to each. I do not think they
> will sing to me.
>   (*Norton Anthology*, p. 226, v. 120-125)

Here we can feel the disturbing agonies of self pity because the process of aging, like the merciless movement of the cosmic seasons, is inescapable. A self pity that seems to imply a mutation of affirmation and negation which may provoke the question: Why these moanings? There is, imbedded in these lines, a desperate sense of regret particularly if that person's life was not fully self actualized. Helen Johnson, however, is not alone in wallowing in regret and self pity. Even John Keats moaned and agonized over what death would deprive him in his poem, *"When I have Fears That I May Cease To Be*:

> When I have fears that I may
> cease to be.
> Before my pen has gleaned my
> teeming brain.
> Before high piled books in character
> Hold like rich garners the full
> ripened grain.
>   (*Norton Anthology*, p. 807, v. 4-14)

Here we feel sorry for Keats at the fullness of his life being afraid that he will never utilize his full potential before he dies. Keats here, unashamed of self love, recognizes his own talents in ("my teeming brain") but death may deprive him the chance to produce books of high priced poetry. His choice of words like, "my teeming brain," "like rich garners" and "full ripened grain" have a delicious sadness because Keats pulls the reader along with his frustrations and doubts by promoting a haunting sense of loss not only for himself but the society. And so, like John Keats and Helen Johnson's poem: *Invocation* seems to have the same frustrations, doubts, hopes and even desires.

The poem opens with a plea for the physical vegetation that the poet loves to remain eternal. This life (Life after Death) should be taken over and represented by the blossoming vegetations:

> Let me be buried in the rain
> In a deep, dripping wood,
> Under the worm breast of Earth.
> (*Norton Anthology*, p. 13-17, v. 1-4)

In this piece, we see her yearning for eternity in the "rain," the "deep dripping woods," the "Warm earth" which recalls the fertility and the life-giving attributes of the earth that has a motherly sustaining nature. This search for eternity, a craving for eternal continuity of passions, is relayed in:

> And paint a picture on my
> tomb
> with dirt and a piece of
> bough, of a girl and a boy
> beneath a ripe, round moon
> Eating of love with eager spoon
> and vowing, an eager vow.
> (Ibid p. 317, v. 5-8)

At this point in the poem, a reader is almost intoxicated by the flow of the craving for an everlasting sexual intimacy with its life-giving energy that should never end. But at another point also in the poem, the African side of me shivers at the thought of placing an erotic picture of sexual intimacy on a tomb! Is this all she wants to be remembered for? The love of erotic sex? Will this offer a sort of edification for posterity? But who says that poetic inspiration ought to have a rational systematic path? Even William Wordsworth, in his definition of poetic emotions, did not give us a criteria, a yard stick for the appropriate overflow of powerful emotions. It is the thought that counts. This powerful craving for eternity is evoked again in her prescriptions for the state or condition of the surroundings of her tomb:

> But let the weed, the flower, the tree
> Riotous, rampant, wild and free
> Grow high above my head.
> (Ibid p. 1318, v. 11-13)

This is the story of exuberance, of joy, of ecstacy, of jouissance, that should live after the demise of the body. This sounds almost as a clarion call for nature to rejoice after her death. A poem that recalls John Donne's poem: *Death Be Not Proud*. There is a jubilant underlined feeling here that so long as the vegetation continues to blossom, her life will also continue even in her absence. The ironic twist here is in the representation of an absence in its presence.

Magalu

Octavio Paz in discussing the problems of modernity and poetry in his book: *The Other Voice*, defines poetry as:

> An incessant zig-zagging rebellion against doctrines and churches. But at the same time, no less constant love of humiliated reality, scorning the manipulations of fatism and speculations of rationalism. Poetry: The Stone of Scandal of Modernity. (p. 15)

In the above piece, Paz in his usual warmness shows the unstructured hostility of poetry towards organized church doctrines as well as the manipulations between the church and philosophic rationalism. Poetry's negations of organized religion is due to the tendency of religion to control and manipulate the members of a group, while poetry's essential strength comes from freedom and the perpetual craving for that freedom.

Secondly, poetry's essential spirit, the spirit of imagination, passion, intuition and spontaneity, are completely antithetical to that spirit of philosophic rationalism (science) which seems to crave facts and the logic of those facts. It is because of this propensity of poetry to ride against science and organized religion that Paz brands it: The Stone of the Scandal of Modernity. We do not need to enter into the etymological or semantic implications/complications, dennotations/connotations of this branding of poetry. But, suffice to say that modernity is not necessarily scandalous, nor is all poetry mainly about modernity. And the word modernity! How does one define it, since it is so elusive, bewitching, diabolical with a perpetual tendency to escape definitions. We shall leave this branding of poetry for discussions in another context.

However, this small hint by Paz of poetry's seemingly unstructured negations of organized religion and philosophic rationalism is necessary for us to understand Helen Johnson's Poem: *Magalu*. The poem *Magalu* seems to be a silent indictment of religion because religion tends to deprive the human being of his/her joys of a dance, of sexual bliss and all other cravings of human appetite. Johnson, in this poem, gives us a setting that is spirited, dizzy with agitation of all wild and living things. The best and worst in nature are alive and fully energized. We see this liveliness in the zig zag that hovers over the greedy mouth of the crocodile. This liveliness goes on in the vulture that "bears away the foolish jackal." Even the bird, flamingo, has improved its beauty to "a dash of Pink" and its beauty is gorgeously symmetrical because "against dark green mangroves the slender legs" of the flamingo rivals "her slim neck." The lake is personified, given human attributes because it is "bustling with "laughter" and "music that lulls the lizard to sleep." This is a happy, enchanting, idyllic summer day when all nature seems joyful and boisterous. The sort of joy that would be contagious to a passionate lover of nature and even solitude. This joyful setting of a warm summer day, should remind the reader of T.S. Eliot's bitter joy in his: *The Burial of the Dead.* where:

> April is the cruelest month,
> breeding lilacs out of the
> dead land, mixing memory
> and desire, stirring
> dull roots with spring rain,
> Winter kept us warm, covering
> Earth in forgetful snow,
> feeding
> A little life with
> dried tubers. (p. 2267, v. 1-7)

This piece, at first reading inflicts a sense of shock on a reader because Eliot has completely twisted and turned the proverbial joy of the seasons upside down. In his sad, melancholy, he seems to feel that humanity is going through so much decadence that we have lost our sense of taste, discrimination and even desire. But, ironically Eliot seems to be displaying the same morbidity and melancholy that he brands the modern life. That is why he turns the seasonal joys that man gets from nature upside down. That is why April, the beginning of spring, the genesis of seasonal joys, turns out in Eliot's mind to be less pleasant. Spring, to Eliot, is less desirable because it provokes sad and morbid memories that are better left alone. But for Eliot, winter, the death of the year, turns out to be more pleasant because it covers memories, while feeding little life with dried tubers." What kind of food can these insects, these worms get from dried tubers? But this is Eliot's world. A world of decadence, of sterility and pessimism about human life at this period in history! But not for Helen Johnson.

Johnson, in the poem *Magalu*, believes that the only thing that diverts human attention from the joy, the happiness, the full participation in the paradise of nature on earth is Christianity. It is for this belief that she is bent on persuading her friend, Magalu, to stay away from Christianity. Her appeal and plea to her friend are playful and almost delirious like the symphonic metaphors in her utterance:

> In such a place,
> In this pulsing, riotous gasp
> of color,
> I met Magalu, dark as a tree
> at night,
> Eager-lipped, listening to a man
> with a white color
> And a small black book with a
> cross on it.
> Oh Magalu, come! Take my hand
> and I will read you poetry,
> chromatic words,
> Seraphic symphonies,
> Fill up your throat with laughter
> and your heart with song.
> Do not let him lure you
> from your laughing waters,
> lulling lakes, lissome winds.
> Would you sell the colors of
> your sunset and the fragrance
> of your flowers, and the
> passionate wonder of your
> forest for a creed that will
> not let you dance?

This section of the poem is subdued, but delirious like the intoxicating melody of a symphony. In a tone of frightened anticipation, the poet appeals to her friend to stay away from that man with a bible because of all other associated negations of Christianity. A religion that seems to be anti-life itself. And Magalu, the friend, suddenly finds herself caught (like a new convert) between the pull of two competing pleasures. The pleasure from the world (joyful, blissful, happy) and Christianity (heaven-bound) but sterile and even stale. For Magalu, the worldly pull seems to succeed as the poet offers a hand and pulls her in to enjoy poetry. A song from heaven, a paradise melody, a symphony of angels (Seraphine). A song that because of its delicious delicacy fills "the throat with laughter," joy, ecstacy, jouissance, bliss. And to consolidate her fears of Christian negations, the poet warns her friend in:

> Do not let him lure you
> from your laughing waters,
> lulling lakes, lissome winds.

At this point in the poem, the poet is imploring the friend not to be lured away from the simple happiness of nature, like seeing the joy and bliss of the boisterous and enchanting laugher of the lake. This is delirious and almost intoxicating like the lulling lakes and lissome winds.

However, the beauty of this poem comes from the fact that this lure of the worldly happiness on Magalu is diametrically opposed to the lure of Christianity. These competing pulls between heaven and the lure of the world are what Saint Augustine warns about in his two books: *The Confessions* and *The City of God*.

In "The Confessions," Saint Augustine describes this intoxicating attraction by worldly joys such as stealing grapes from farms, his excessive womanizing and wanton sexual escapades. But while he was pulled by the world, his mother was also pulling him towards God, through her prayers and intercessions. Thanks to his mother, Monica, he became one of the greatest Christians of all time. But even Augustine—in all his holiness, in all his glory—had one sin that he would have liked to hide from himself and even from God. That sin was his illegitimate son, Adeodatus. It is of interest to note that in his confessions, he spent ten passages describing the childish pranks of stealing grapes and yet spent only five sentences discussing his illegitimate son. There are several explanations for this behavior. But this text is not a treatise like Sade's "Friends of the Society of Crime."

Helen Johnson's *Magalu*, had the same pull between the world and the heavenly persuasion by that man with the bible. And if we stretch our imagination (knowing the morals of today's preachers) it is quite possible that man with the bible may have ulterior motives which maybe to pull Magalu to God, or teach her the philosophy in the bedroom. And even the poet's motives insinuated in her description of Magalu as:

> dark as a tree at night
> Eager-lipped

may have sexual insinuations.

However, I do not think that Magalu (like all men/women) listened to Saint Augustine's whispers beyond the ages in his book: "The City of God." In this book, Augustine insisted that faithful Christians could live side by side with sinners and yet not sin because of our faith. And that the goodness of God toward his faithful servants is so strong, powerful and even contagious to a point that it will eventually override the power of evil. The critical question then is: for Magalu, what would have been the better choice between these competing pleasures?

Johnson, as if in anticipation of an answer to the above question is relentless in pounding and compounding the beatitudes of the world against that of the Christian preacher in:

> Would you sell the colors of
> Your sunset and the fragrance
> Of your flowers, and the
> Passionate wonder of your
> Forest,
> For a creed that will
> Not let you dance?

This section of the poem shows that the poet has stepped into a higher ladder of poetic inspiration because of the passionate intensity of her thought, the delicate, delicious purity and sweetness of her meaning to a point where you are forced to scream: More! More words, please more! No reader of this poem, mesmerized by such emotional intensity, will fail to believe that William Wordsworth's dictum for Romantic poetry which was that: Poetry is emotions recollected in tranquility or the overflow of powerful emotions has been fully satisfied. But her poem: "Bottled: New York," tells a different story.

Bottled: New York

T.S. Eliot, wondering about the role of Christianity to new converts, remarked in his poem: *The Journey of the Magi*, that:

> We return to our places,
> This kingdoms,
> No longer at ease,
> In this old dispensation,
> With an alien people still
> Clutching at their gods.

One of the concerns of Eliot in that poem is the problem of displacement and the trauma of dealing with that displacement in the case of a new Christian convert who must be confronted with the pain of dealing with divided loyalties: The loyalty to his former ways of life and his former friends who themselves have not changed. How would the new convert do it! This notion of displacement seems to be the central theme of the poem: *Bottled: New York*:

> Upstairs on the third floor
> of the 135th Street Library
> In Harlem, I saw a little
> Bottle of sand, brown sand
> Just like the kids make pies
> out of down at the beach.
> But the label said: This sand
> was taken from the Sahara desert!
> Imagine that! The Sahara desert!
> Some bozo's been all the way
> to Africa to get some sand.

Anyone who has been to New York will remember a city of tall, inhuman buildings, crowded streets, teeming with crowds that jostle for space with cars. The area of Harlem or even Manhattan is devoid of trees, grass or even sand. It should therefore really be a shock for one to find a bottle of sand from the Sahara Desert (Africa) on the third floor of the library. What could possibly be the explanation for this? There are several explanations for this bottle of sand. The most obvious is that it is a souvenir that reminds the owner of the natural world of Africa. A world that is so far (and alien) to New York that it may pass for Jerusalem! Secondly, the owner of this sand may need the sand to teach a lesson in the geography of Africa, with her land mass, people and vegetation. Thirdly, maybe, he needed the sand to teach ecology to people, to show what happens to a vegetation when the eco system is drastically fractured. But whatever his motive, the sand from the Sahara Desert is so much displaced in a city of tall buildings and blaring car horns.

However, my only concern in this poem is why the poet terms this man: "some bozo," because of his curiosity and the sense of adventure. Is this man foolish, insane for bringing a souvenir from Africa! Ironically the only "bozo" in this case could be the one who does not see the thrill and excitement (for souvenirs) from trips and adventures. There is lurking in that statement about the (bozo) some me/them syndrome, (an alienation) from Africa that I can not discuss now!

This sense of displacement, of alienation and the self denigration in the (me/them) syndrome, spills through the second stanza of the poem. Here the logic of the narrative is that the black man, the "Negro dressed fit to kill in yellow gloves and swallow-tail coat and twirling a cane" was over dressed. And being black and dressed like that in Harlem he is displaced and fit only for the jungles of Africa:

> But say, I was where I could see his
> face,
> and somehow, I could see him
> dancing in a jungle,
> A real honest-to-goodness jungle,
> and he wouldn't have on them
> Trick clothes—those yellow shoes
> and yellow gloves
> And swallow-tail coat.
> He wouldn't have on nothing.
> And he wouldn't be carrying no
> cane.
> He would be carrying a *spear*
> with a *sharp fine* point
> Like the bayonets we had "over
> there"
> And the end would be *dipped*
> in some kind of *Hoo doo Poison*.
> And he would be dancing black
> and *naked* and gleaming.

And he would have *rings* in his
ears and on his nose.
And *bracelets* and *necklaces* of
elephant's teeth.
Gee, I bet he would be beautiful then
all right. (v. 1-14)

The passage above contains a sense of bitter humor. But the idea that a black and female poet should display such self castigating denigration on what Achebe for lack of a better word called: Anti-racist, racism is disconcerting. It is also interesting that a black man who may have worked hard to buy himself a pair of beautiful clothes is ridiculed and compared to the savage massai running about naked in the wild savagery in Africa. The poet in her bitter humor paints this innocent dancer with an elaborate anatomy of a massai warrior, a savage, running about in the bush naked. We see this bitter humor and ridicule in:

I could see him dancing in a jungle.
A real honest-to-goodness jungle.

The question here is why is a black man properly dressed in his Elizabethan outfit good only for the African jungle rather than Harlem, New York? This kind of negation, this negative stigma, this scourge should remind the reader of that social degradation in: Can anything good come out of Nazareth? But something good did come out, at least for the Christians: A Savior was born. And as if to over kill, to grind her black brother in greater mud, the poet continues her verbal lynching in:

He would have on nothing.
And he wouldn't be carrying no
cane.
He would be carrying a spear
with a sharp point,
like the bayonets we have
"over there."
And the end would be dipped
in some kind of Hoodoo Poison.
And he would be dancing black
and naked and gleaming.
And he would have rings in his

ears and on his nose.
And bracelets and necklaces of
elephant teeth.
Gee, I bet he would be beautiful
then all right.

The above piece appears to be the most disdainful, degrading, "low down" portrayal of a black man that I have ever read in print. The poet in this piece is not only satisfied in stripping this dancer of his humanity and social standing, she had to physically strip him naked, but hand him a sharp, poisoned spear, so that this dancer is not only dancing naked and gleaming, he is also dangerously menacing even in his entertainment. However, what is sad and even disconcerting is that all the multiple forms of degradation are not just restricted to the dancer, but actually directed and showered on Africa. This poet sees Africa and Africans as dangerously savage beasts who run about naked in the bush with gleaming black bodies and menacing sharp, poisoned spears. This must be a sign of addiction to *National Geographic*. The most disturbing concern from this poem is that (me/them) syndrome, the (civilized/savage) syndrome where the African American in Harlem is civilized while the African in the continent is seen as a menacing savage. And as if in savage relief, the poet looks at the contortions of this brutal, verbal lynching and she exhales a self depreciating sigh in:

Gee, I bet he would be beautiful
Then all right.

Amen to this sense of revulsion.
But, perhaps we can not avoid to ask the question that will seem to tie together the crucial, but dramatic logic of the poem. That question is: Why is the dancer's outfit labeled as—

Trick Clothes—those
Yellow shoes and yellow
Gloves,
And swallow-tail coat.

They are "trick clothes" because a black man at this period of American history, dressed in a gentleman's Elizabethan outfit, is so thoroughly out of place in Harlem as the sand from the Sahara Desert, stored on the third floor of a library in New York. So, if Harlem is not a suitable place for this gentleman dancer, why is he fit to be a savage Massai warrior, running wild in the jungle with a sharp, poisoned, menacing spear! That joke is no longer funny! It smacks with bitterness and contempt.

The Road

Helen Johnson's poem: *The Road* excites me because Wole Soyinka, the Nigerian Nobel Prize winner in Literature in (1986) wrote a poem with the same title. So, in this piece, we will examine how both poets treated this title in terms of concrete meaning, mythical and philosophical. For Soyinka, the road has multiple names, layers with different dennotations/connotations, implications/complications that are all mixed in the African Yoruba, mythology. A mythology that is similar to that of the Incas in Latin America. The kind that Mircea Eliade calls the "eternal return."

Soyinka's Road also ties in with the pantheism of Leopold Senghor, the Nobel Prize winner in Literature and former President of Senegal in West Africa. Senghor, in his pantheism claims that: The African universe is unique. That from God through man to the smallest grain of sand is a seamless whole. But the road for Helen Johnson, is not just a trail to drive through, it is a metaphor for the social and political progression of the black race. Helen's Road does not extend beyond this world. Soyinka's does because the road of life for Soyinka links man to man, God to man, man to his ancestors. It is a vicious cycle, a wheel of fortune that turns round and round *ad infinitum*. Let us at this point, examine Soyinka's concept of the Road taken from his poem: *Death in the Dawn:*

> The right fool for joy, the left
> dread
> And the mother prayed,
> child, may you never walk
> when the road waits famished.
> Traveler you must set forth
> at dawn
> I promise marvels of the holy hour
> presages as the white cock's flapped
> perverse impalement—as who

would dare
The wrathful wings of man's
progression C
But such another wraith!
Brother, silenced in the startled
hug of your invention—
is this mocked grimace.
This closed contortion
—I? (v. 1-10)

In this verse, Soyinka takes an ordinary story of a car accident which resulted in the fatalities of a man and a white cock and weaves it into a subtle poetic myth of local and universal proportions. The first of these myths about –"Left foot for dread and right for joy" is a local myth which claims that when you start out on a journey on foot and you stumble on a stump, first, with your left foot, it's a sign that your journey may have bad luck. Where as if you stumbled first with your right foot, then that journey may have good luck and joy. It is because of the awful mysterious and yet unavoidable repercussions of this myth, that every mother should pray for her child's safety every time a child travels. This myth may have started in Africa! We do not know. But it is a universal truth that every mother wishes her child well, every time he/she travels. This is how a local myth attains universal recognition because a mother's feeling for her child is universal. The third myth is more complicated because the road is not just a trail to travel. The road is also a symbol of a "god" who because (she/he) supplies humans a means of communication, he/she should be fed as a means of appeasement. If not, he/she may take what we value highly, like our children and the white cock in a car accident. Accidents, according to Yoruba mythology, occur because the road (god) is hungry when man becomes careless sometimes and does not feed this god. So, in this poem, the poet hints that to make a joyful, successful journey, the traveler should first sacrifice chicken or animals to this god under the prayerful and watchful eyes of his/her mother, so as to have good luck! But, in case you forgot this ritual, you should make your journey very early in the morning, when some white cock may have been sacrificed inadvertently before you arrived.

However, in the journey discussed in this poem, even though a white cock had been sacrificed in an accident does not seem to have been enough. It did not appease or satisfy the hunger of this ravenous god. That is why he/she took the next man's life in that fatality on the road.

So, at the scene of this car crash where a man has been killed, the poet goes into a melancholy mood, of soul searching, only to discover the horrible evil that comes out of man's good invention of the automobile, the: Car. A car which now behaves like that proverbial African hunter's dog that goes mad and runs after its own master! How can this be? The car, like the dog, is supposed to be man's best friend! But how mistaken!! So, in the mind of the poet, man is the author of his own misery. That is why the poem ends in that chilling shock and bewilderment:

But such another wraith!
Brother, silenced in the startled
Hug of your invention—
Is this mocked grimace.
This closed contortion—*I*.

In the above verse, the word "wraith" has condensed layers of metaphysical poetic conceit. At one level, it is a floral arrangement placed at the tomb of the dead. But in the context of the poem, man is sacrificed as a wraith to appease a hungry and angry god. And this man was sacrificed in that accident in that "startled hug of your invention." An accident that reduced man into a heap of rubbish, of that "mocked grimace and the closed contortions." Ironically this is what (>I'), man, has done to myself, the poet seems to remark! The "I" at the end of the poem is not innocent, singular or individual. It is a universal "I" that includes (You and I) all of humanity who made this invention. This is how Soyinka weaves a local, single myth, into universal proportions. As we have seen, Soyinka's myth of the *Road* has condensed layers of implications, dennotations/connotations. But Helen Johnson's: *The Road*, has different sets of significations.

Johnson's Road entails not only a concrete trail, but also a symbol of the social and political progressions of the black race!

The Road
Ah, little road, all whirry in the
breeze,
A leaping clay hill lost among trees,
The bleeding note of rapture—steaming
thrust
caught in a drowsy bush

> And stretched out in a single singing
> line of dusky song.
> Ah, little road, brown as my race
> is brown,
> Your trodden beauty like our trodden
> pride,
> Dust of the dust, they must not
> bruise you down.
> Rise to one brimming golden,
> spilling cry! (v. 1-9)

The poem seems to suggest that the poet, who has been away in the city for a while, was now returning home to the country for a visit. That is why we have that sigh of relief as she travels this country trail with the wind (breeze) blowing in her hair and ear. We hear this relief in the "Oh little road, all whirry in the breeze." We can almost see the poet in our mind's eye as she trails the small country road of "leaping clay" meandering along the hill to the entertainment of the music from country birds. It sounds like an idyllic story of nostalgia. The nostalgia of a journey into the country on vacation, from school or just on a visit.

Then very soon, just immediately, this joyful journey, this journey through an idyllic world, changes tone and reminiscences by running smack into political realities of the times. It is like waking up from a beautiful dream into a nightmare! And in politics, the story is the same! It is a story of frustration, of mutilation, of anxiety, of hope, pain, doubt and desire. In a beautiful evocation, the road takes on a metaphor of a suffering people with all their associated sufferings. In that suffering, we see people whose pride, dignity, joy, culture, song and language has been trodden and bruised. And as the journey progresses, the poet, deep in thought, saturated with anxiety, seems to be struck with that last flame of inspiration. The kind that struck the prophet Isaiah on his way to Jerusalem or those crowds on Pentecost Sunday. So, she breaks out, screaming: "Rise to one brimming golden, spilling cry! As a reader, one is struck with shock or almost intoxicated with the beauty of that thought and even more beautiful, in its execution. That command to "rise to one brimming golden, spilling cry," was not given to the road. The road has no life. It is inanimate! And so, in one swift semantic change, it is the metaphor, the double, the mirror dance of the real thing, that takes up this banner to blaze the trail of freedom! Nobody does it better than Helen Johnson. Helen Johnson's poem, *The Road*, celebrates the road as a trail to drive through, but more importantly, as a metaphor of the struggles of the black race and their progressive suffering. But Wole Soyinka's poem: *The Road*, celebrates the road as a trail, myth, god, as a medium that links man to the spirit world, to his ancestors and to God, Himself. Helen's *Road* stops in this world, at the theatre of battle, while Soyinka's paradigm is purely transcendental!

Chapter 4

Gwendolyn Bennett

> I shall hate you
> like a dart of singing steel
> shot through still air
> at even-tide.
> *Hatred*

In our introduction, we discussed the different uses of poetry between the men and women of Harlem Renaissance. That for the men, poetry served as a war song from the mountain top. But for the women, poetry was for poetry full of passion, joy and the soul of the Black race. Gwendolyn Bennett was one of these women who wrote poetry for poetry that was sometimes full of nostalgia for Africa, the ugly union between Black beauty and slavery and even simplistic topics like hatred and retribution.

In her poem, *Heritage*, Bennett is confronted by the disturbing conflict between her craving for Africa and the negation of that craving. In this poem, a reader is immediately confronted with images of Africa as seen from the beautiful palm trees, the sweet flow of the river Nile, with its life-sustaining power. But this spiritual or mental flight to Africa becomes a simple farce because the poet does not seem to be fully engaged in the sincerity of the craving:

> I want to hear the chanting
> around a heathen fire of a strange
> Black race.
> (*Norton Anthology*, p. 1228, v. 10-12)

The above piece must convey some cold, detached, distant narrative of a feigned craving for Africa because it lacks sincerity and a serious engagement with her cravings. In fact, Africa may be a continent that the poet really despises because she refers to her in those disturbing, disdainful words with loaded condescending, debasing, denigrations. A reader's fears are aroused by such phrases as "chanting around a heathen fire," "a strange Black race." These phrases seem to convey a sense of alienation and even distrust. And the word heathen is so very subjective and condescending, particularly because of the obvious insinuations of the (primitive, pagan), a negation of civilization. There is also that disturbing reference to Africa as ("A strange Black race") which has all the ugly insinuations of separation (me/them) and even some implied inferiority of that strange Black race when compared to the writer. And because of the absence of a sincere craving for Africa, her poetic flirtations with the river Nile, with all the lotus and stars, appear as sentimental, dreamy journeys of a wondering heart. Bennett's concentration, her anxieties, her hopes seem to be else where.

Her poetic feelings in this poem seem directed at her anxieties, doubts, hopes and even desires of the Black race as they trade comedy, Buffoonery-minstrel shows for the recognition of a small slice of human dignity. A dignity that could not be achieved except through another indignation of compounding a negation on negation. This negation on negation comes from the fact that these minstrel shows are a negation and affirmation of happiness because they serve only as a mirror suppression of anger with fake smiles. And this is a topic that the poet could have nourished and nurtured for serious poetic effect. But she does not. So, when she tries to juggle her engagement between a theme that she loves with the one she despises, her poem appears weak because of the lack of a systematic thought process:

> I want to feel the surging of my sad people's soul, Hidden by a minstrel smile.
> (Ibid p. 1228, v. 16-18)

Here again is that display of a craving and not a fully committed engagement in: "I want to feel the surging," which really implies a lack of feeling. Perhaps if the poet had read Langston Hughes: *Mother to Son*, she may have gotten a grounding on how to treat commitment. These minstrel shows, because of their mutation of affirmation/negation, of anger/joy, laughter/crying would have been her most effective poetic tool to enunciate Black frustrations because they would inadvertently have ignited the flavors of those Yeatsian images of the Dancer and the Dance.

Bennet, however, seems to me to be a more serious poet, particularly in her treatment of the beauty of a Black woman than Anne Spencer. My reason for this judgement is because while Bennett is concerned with a thought process that would produce tensions and contentions in a reader, Spencer was concerned only with the delicate sexual sweetness of that beauty. Bennett proves this point in her poem: *To a Black Girl*.

In this poem, Bennett seems more successful than the poem *Heritage* because of a cogent thought process that is systematically developed. This poem, in the spirit of Negritude, evokes the natural beauty of a dark girl, leading from her beautiful dark breasts, the breaking sadness of her voice, to her wayward eye-lids. This progression of thought about her beauty gains intensity when the poet unleashes a juxtaposition of this free beauty, this queenly demeanor with the scourged memory of slavery with all the associated connotations/denotations of pain. This girl is certainly:

> Something of the old forgotten queens
> lurks in the little abandon of your walk
> and something of the shackled slave
> sobs in the rhythm of your talk.
>   (*Norton Anthology*, p. 1228, v. 5-8)

The persona in this poem displays that free and relaxed gait of a queen. But in this relaxed demeanor lurks the buried sadness of the scourge of a slave. The intensity in the poem is increased by the biting competing passions: The passion of a beautiful black girl and the passions of a slave who is also beautiful. The poignant beauty of this verse is in the fact that one can not separate the queen who is beautiful, from the slave who is also as beautiful as a queen. This section of the poem should immediately evoke W.B. Yeat's chestnut tree in *Among School Children*:

> Oh chestnut tree,
> great rooted blossomed,
> are you the leaf, the blossom or
> the bole,

Oh body swayed by music,
Oh brightening smile,
How can we know the
Dancer from the Dance?
   (*Norton Anthology*, p. 1979, v. 60-69)

The beauty of this poem is that it invites the reader playfully to observe the joy of competing passions, which should be similar to the beauty of the slave who also happens to be a queen. And from this beautiful poem, the reader moves gradually to confront the scourge of the poem: *Hatred*.

In "Hatred," we watch the disturbing cold, calculated antiques of a terrorist with his cold, dark dart of singing steel that inflicts merciless punishment with cold hands. As the victim yearns for freedom, this tormentor with wicked, fiendish eyes unleashes more punishment with the sting of cold, merciless, steel arrows. This hatred and the corresponding punishment are inflicted because of some past wrongs. This is a dreadful anatomy of hatred with the calculated systematic reprisals that are even more haunting because they are seen as a game. But to really appreciate this poem, we have to visit the scene of terror:

I shall hate you like a dart of singing steel,
shot through still air at evening tide.
   (*Norton Anthology*, p. 1229, v. 1-4)

At the beginning of this poem, the poet reveals the cold, calculated anatomy of hatred with the concomitant punishment. This hatred is compared to a dart of hard steel, shot when the weather is calm, so that the dart would do the most damage because of the absence of friction from the wind. The singing steel evokes the malicious laughter of a terrorist at the sufferings of his victims. The poignancy of this hatred is revealed in comparing it to a game. A game of torture that the protagonist enjoys because she picks the time and the manner of inflicting this pain for the greatest effect. The effectiveness of this poem is in the systematic and almost organic expectation and progression of thought which pulls the reader gradually through the anxieties hopes and desires of a victim, who because of saturation with pain, may try to escape. But for this victim, there is no escape. No escape because when:

Your heart will yearn for the lonely splendors of the tree;
while rekindled fires in my eyes shall wound you like swift arrows
    (Ibid v. 11-16)

In this piece, the victim is trapped, tortured and prepared for the burning sacrifice. The terror, the state of mind of this victim, maybe reminiscent of that pathetic moaning and yearning of the Greek Sybil in: *I Yearn to Die*. The beauty of this poem is not only in the systematic progression of thought. It is in the poet's understanding of the internal monologues not only of the executioner, but also the victim as it pertains to their mutual anxieties, frustrations, hopes, doubts and desires. And the desire for this cold, calculated punishment comes as a price for some past wrongs:

Memory will lay it's hands upon your breast
And you will understand my hatred.
    (Ibid v. 18-20)

Here at last, we know why the victim can not escape punishment even in death. This is all because even death can not escape death because memory (the harbinger of history) survives eternity.

Chapter 5

Angelina Grimke

> I have just seen a beautiful thing
> slim and still,
> against a gold, gold sky,
> A straight cypress,
> sensitive
> Exquisite.
> *The Black Finger*

Angelina Grimke was one of the sturdy Black women of Harlem Renaissance who wrote poetry for poetry, on a variety of topics like the scourge of winter or the tenderness of spring. Sometimes she ventured into eroticism as we see in, *The Black Finger* or the enormity of Black threat against White repression that we see in *Tenebris*. Her most memorable poems seem to be: *The Winter Twilight*; *The Black Finger*, *When the Green Lies Over the Earth* and *Tenebris*.

Her poem: *The Winter Twilight*, is a demonstration of the scourging effect of winter on a vegetation, the fields and the environment. The poem gains intensity by the juxtaposition of opposites such as, silence/ death against whispers, sighs and breath, thereby evoking that Yeatsian image of the Dancer and the Dance. But despite the dreariness of the season, the trees lean towards the sky which has a green gold color, reminiscent of the richness of hope even from a universe that is beyond our control or even understanding. But to really understand and appreciate the thought process in the poem, we have to visit:

> A silence slipping around like death,
> you chased by a whisper, a sigh,

a breath;
one group of trees lean, naked and
cold,
Inking their crest against a
Sky green-gold;
One path that knows where the corn
flowers were;
Lonely, apart, unyielding, on fir;
And over it softly leaning down,
One star that I loved ere the
fields went down.
>(*Norton Anthology of African
>American Literature*, p. 944, v. 1-5)

From the above verse, one can almost listen to the sigh of silence, like whispering pines on a sad, cold, tree that is tormented by winter. But harsh as this winter appears, the trees look hopefully to the sky that has a green, gold color. A sign of the richness of hope! This juxtaposition of the cold foreboding winter trees against the seeming joy in the heavens should naturally intensify man's helplessness. This winter does not torment only the trees, but also the cornfields whose flowers whither in the cold. There is embedded in this verse, a nagging sense of exasperation as the poet seems to crave a return to spring in: "One star that I love ere the fields went down." But this craving for spring remains only a wish, because seasons, naturally roll on with or without human intervention. After experiencing the agonies of a winter scourge in this poem, we move gradually to *The Black Finger*, which seems to have some erotic insinuations.

This poem, *The Black Finger*, has implications of sexual eroticism because the beautiful finger pointing upwards seems to recall the erection of the male penis. We shall observe this point from the poem:

The Black Finger
I have just seen a beautiful thing
slim and still
Against a gold, gold sky
A straight cypress
sensitive
exquisite,
A Black Finger

> pointing upwards.
> Why, beautiful, still finger are
> you black?
> And why are you pointing upwards?
> > (*Norton Anthology of African*
> > *American Literature*, p. 944, v. 1-8)

The setting in that poem is sexual, erotic, pornographic, but exciting. It is exciting because it seems to recall a sexual scene where a woman observes her male partner before sexual intimacy. It is a pornographic scene that seems to provoke a breaking alertness. But the point of real interest in the poem is in the second to the last line where the poet, mesmerized by the sight, the erotic sensuality of the male penis, poses a rhetorical question:

> why, beautiful, still finger are you black?

The implication of that question is that the color black seems to corrupt and spoil everything because of its association with impurities, ugliness and slavery. The poet here seems to lament that even sexual bliss and enjoyment maybe adulterated by the blackness of this male penis that is so "slim and still," "straight as a cypress," "sensitive" and really "exquisite." And the answer to the question: (Why are you pointing upwards?) will be quite easy if you have a sensitive mind. The answer of course is that it is pointing upwards because it craves a female penetration, a female sexual embrace! If we have been teased by the pornographic insinuations in this poem, we can now tenderly embrace the sweet fragrance of spring in a poem called: *When the Green Lies Over the Earth*.

In this poem, we meet the loving tenderness that seems to grow more in spring, the youth of the year. This youthful love, this tenderness that seems to be so contagious shows in the "wooing" of birds in their "restless feet," their "chirrups," "thrills" and "songs." We feel this tenderness in the blossoming daisies at the feet of a lover. But this youthful love seemed to be abused and even over used because:

> For you have sung and have prayed
> and pled.
> This many, many a year
> And the blossom fall.

On the garden wall
And drift like snow on the
green below.
>   (*Norton Anthology of African
>   American Literature*, p. 944, v. 20-23)

Here is a demonstration of a wasted love affair. Here is a love without feelings, so that the beauty simply floated to ruin because of the lack of care and commitment. This love therefore begins to crumble and decay. And at this point in the poem, Grimke infuses her love of opposites for tension and poetic intensity as seen in the budding roses with sharp thorns. This poem carries and displays some competing passions which rise and fall naturally. We see these competing passions in the beautiful green of spring that turns to snow, the human love that bleeds out of necessity for lack of nurturing, and even the beautiful rose has a sharp thorn. These juxtapositions of opposites intensify the tension in the poem because of the mutual pull of these opposites. Also because of the wasted nature of this love, the lover's heart no longer leaps at sunset glow. That glow was a dance of youth. A dance of spring when love was fresh and almost self sustaining like the blossoming spring. This poem is a classic case of a mechanically successful poem because the metaphors, the running themes and structures are carefully and systematically woven together. But despite this mechanical success, there is something that seems to be lacking in Grimke's poems. That thing is the "overflow of powerful emotions." This lack of emotional intensity makes her poems pale, sterile and even starved of feeling. One of these poems without feelings is: *Tenebris*.

The poem, *Tenebris*, is a poem in search of meaning because the poet gives no clues except the huge Black hand with long fingers that pluck at the bricks of the Whiteman's house. However, the poem has structural beauty which is not only in the mystery, but in the enormity of the symbol which may also convey an ominous terror that may be inflicted by the Black race on the Whites even in the seeming sanctuary of their brick houses. The small bricks are the color of blood because they will be a very inadequate defense against the pending Black wrath that may turn a sanctuary into a blood bath. This poem that seems written against itself, written in search of meaning, somehow unleashes an interesting rhetorical question in,

Is it a Black hand or a
Shadow?
> (*Norton Anthology African
> American Literature*, p. 1927, v. 11-14)

Here is a rhetorical question that the poet does not seriously demand an answer. But, as with all rhetorical questions, the question may be the answer and the answer may be the question. At another level, the question may be the answer because the impending threat of the Black race on Whites may be real (Black hand) or feigned (shadow). But the threat is real enough.

To Clarissa Scot Delany

This poem must be a requiem, a song of the living for the dead. The poet mourns not only the passage of Clarissa, but the passage of all things in nature, the inevitability of this current and the helplessness of man and all living things in the wake of this grinding mill. The poem opens with a double coded statement of admission and even rejection of death:

> She has not found herself a
> hard pillow
> and a long hard bed,
> a chilling cypress, a wan
> willow
> For her gay young head C
> These are for the dead. (p. 15, v. 1-5)

This is a piercing, agonizing and exasperating feeling for the loss of a dear friend or sister. Underlined in those lines is a desperate attempt at rejecting the inevitability of death. Of course, she could not in (death) celebrate her own burial. That is the business of friends and relatives who find her "a hard pillow," "a long hard bed" (her coffin) and the location and burial place, which is around a "chilling cypress, a wan willow." The poet, still in shock, and denial, can not believe Clarissa is actually dead. That is why she claims in a tone of an oxymoron that the dead is not actually dead in dying. That is why all the burial rites in a groove of "chilling cypress, a wan willow for her gay young head . . ." could not be for the dead Clarissa because in the poet's mind, she is not dead because these ceremonies are for the dead and yet not for Clarissa who is dead; but yet not dead in the mind of the poet. And so, in the next stanza, (believe it or not) she must accept the passage and temporal nature of all things which include the life of one so precious as Clarissa.

The poet, overcome with grief, unleashes a tirade of rhetorical questions that she does not seriously expect any answers. And the fascination with rhetorical questions is that the question may be the answer, just as the answer is in the question. So, let us take a joyful interest in examining each of these rhetorical questions:

> Does the violet lidded twilight die?
> And the piercing dawn
> And the white clear moon and the
> night-blue sky . . . ? (v. 6-8)

The above verse really mourns the shortness of human life compared to other things in the cosmos. The "violet lidden twilight" does not die because day turns to night which is constantly repeated in circles. In the same way, "the piercing dawn," "the white clear moon" and "the night-blue sky" does not die! The moon repeats appearances on the average after every thirty days, while the "night-blue sky," changes color only according to the local weather or atmospheric changes. But if the "violet lidden twilight, "the piercing dawn," "the white clear moon" and the "night-blue sky" have a life that repeats in a vicious circle (The poet moans in exasperation) then why is man here today and gone tomorrow like a piece of grass that never comes back when burnt. This is a desperate, agonizing, feeling that tempts one, almost, to question "The goodness of God." And if the last questions dealt with the heavenly bodies with their recycling eternal life, the next questions deal with living things. These questions deal with birds and children whose lives, like man is so limited and temporal:

> Does the shimmering note
> In the shy, shy throat
> of the swaying birds?
> O, does children's laughter
> live not after
> it is heard? (v. 9-14)

The above two verses deal with the temporality of life of the birds and even children's laughter. The shimmering note of the birds stops when the birds die, or when the birds migrate to other locations according to changes in the seasons. Similarly, children's laughter ends when the child stops laughing or when due to some misfortune, that child dies. Here it would appear, quite silently, that the poet may be questioning the fairness of God. Why God gives other things in the universe eternal life, while others are stuck with very short and temporal lives. This part of the poem begins to raise quietly, the great ontological argument about the goodness of God. An argument that has been tackled by theologians from Saint Thomas Aquinas, St. Augustine of Hippo and even C.S. Lewis in his: *The Great Divorce*.

As if to answer the arguments about the goodness of God. The next rhetorical tirades seem to celebrate the nourishing utility of God's sunshine on all living things while the next verse validates the life giving power of rain to all living things on earth including the sea, the flowers, the crushed ferns, clover and even the grass at night:

> Does the dear, dear shine upon your dear, dear
> things
> In the eyes, on the hair
> on waters, on wings
> live no more anywhere?
> Does the tang of the sea, the breath of
> frail flowers,
> of fern crushed, of clover,
> of grass at dark, of the earth
> after showers, not linger, not ever? (v. 15-22)

The obvious answer to that first verse above is yes! The sun in its nourishing, motherly mood, continues to shine and enrich the human eyes, the hair, the water and even strengthens the wings of birds when it rises. And so, like father and mother, the sun and the rain continue their parental obligations, particularly the paternal warm caresses of the rain as it raises the "tang of the sea," giving life to frail "flowers . . . to the crushed fern," the "clover" the "grass at night" and rejuvenation to "the earth" after showers. These two verses seem to recall the boundless love and mercy of God who supplies life to living and non living things through sunshine and the life giving showers of rain. At this point in the poem, the poet seems to turn the reader's attention from the questions about the goodness of God, to the acceptance of God's ultimate design, because God's time is really the best. So, if we believe in God's time and in the goodness of God, we will accept God's ultimate design where nothing on earth seems to last forever. Life is seasonal for plants and vegetations, but temporal for man and animals.

If a reader of this poem believes in the goodness of God and his ultimate holy design, he/she will accept the fact that nothing on earth, even including the vegetation, animals, man and all living things, remain the same. They all change according to this grinding wheel of fortune. So, the answer to the following verse is no! That nothing stays the same. Not even the "beryl in tarns," the "soft orchids" in haze, the "primrose through tree tops," the "unclouded jade of the north sky" and "all the earth's blooms and russets and grays." All simply smudge out and fade. All these plants follow the natural seasons that God had set up. They come and go like the Psalmist spoke about the grasses on the field. And in a tone of sad melancholy, the poet mourns that all the simple thrills and joys in life are all temporal. Even:

> All loveliness, all sweetness
> All grace, all the gay questioning,
> All wonder, all dreaming,
> They that cup beauty that veiled opaled vase
> Are they only the soul of a seeming? (v. 27-30)

The answer to the above nagging questions is no! All essential and even simple joys of man/woman are not meant to last. That is why man sometimes has joy today and sadness the next day.

In a mood of quiet acceptance, the poet proclaims that since human life is full of all these anxieties, frustrations, doubts, hopes and even desires, it was fitting for the precious Clarissa to escape to a new world, a new life: Death.

> O hasn't she found just a little,
> thin door
> And passed through and closed
> it between?
> O aren't those her light feet upon
> that light floor,
>   . . . That her laughter . . .
> O doesn't she lean as we do to

listen? O, doesn't it
mean
she is only unseen, unseen? (v. 31-36)

The above passage is the most haunting, agonizing and exasperating requiem that I have ever read. In a pitch of intense sadness, the poet loudly mourns Clarissa, but at the same time the poet is satisfied that because of Clarissa's eternal goodness, it was only right that she should escape this troubled world to a place of eternal peace. That is why Clarissa in death seemed to have found just a "little thin door" that she passed through and closed behind her. A narrow escape! But escape, all the same! Then comes the scourge of memory. Memory that is a veiled attempt to defeat death by evoking all the associated thrills, reminiscence of her joys, happiness, ecstacy and jouissance. In her attempt to hang on to memory, she could almost (even in death) see Clarissa's light feet upon the light door, listen and hear her laughter, remembering how she leans to listen, and so breaks out in the most tantalizing scream of loss in:

O doesn't it mean
She is only unseen, unseen? (v. 35-36)

And the heart wrenching answer is that she is not simply unseen. She is dead and gone! And in death, there is no return.

Chapter 6

Zora Neal Hurston
Their Eyes Were Watching God:
A Deconstruction

> Jane saw her life like a
> great tree in a leaf with
> things suffered, things enjoyed,
> things done and undone.
> *Their Eyes Were Watching God*:
> A Deconstruction

Several literary theories from Feminism to Deconstruction can be used to read Zora Neal Hurston's novel, Their Eyes Were Watching God. I have decided however, to use the theory and practice of Deconstruction for my readings. But, before I begin my analysis, it is necessary to attempt a definition of Deconstruction. This is only an attempt because definitions according to Kenneth Burke in his, *The Grammar of Motives*, informs us that definitions always fail to carry us to the thingness of things. This is because definitions usually end up teasing us with similes, metaphors, allegories and even catachresis. But despite this dubious nature of defining, I will still attempt it for lack of a better option. Catherine Belsey in her book, *Critical Practice*, defines Deconstruction as:

> The object of deconstructing a text is to examine the process of its production, not the private experiences of the individual author, but the mode of production, the materials and their arrangements in the

> work. The aim is to locate the point of contradiction within the text—composed of contradictions, the text is no longer restricted to a single, harmonious and authoritative reading. Instead it becomes plural, open to re-reading, no longer an object of passive consumption, but an object of work by the reader to produce meaning. (p. 104).

A careful reading of Belsey's definition reveals interesting implications. The first thing that deconstruction eliminates is the biographical flavorings of the author. This is what Roland Barthes refers to in his essay: *The Death of the Author*. But as soon as we eliminate the influence of the author in our readings, language takes up the meaning of the text. But the problem with language is that it has limitless significations and deferment that can go on forever. The second implication of eliminating the influence of the author is that every reader with a language (with various signifiers) brings his reading to bear on a text. This really means that every reader creates a text out of a text. It was based on this brand of reading that Stanley Fish wrote his famous essay: *Is There a Text in This Class*? The answer of course is "no," because every reader writes his own text out of a text. Simply, a poem has as many meanings as the people who read it. Deconstruction therefore is a reader response theory!

But to fully understand deconstruction, we must attempt comparing it with the readings of a classic realist text. This kind of text, Belsey claims: moves inevitably, irreversible to an end, to a conclusion of an ordered series of events to the disclosure of what has been concealed. The realist text is really authoritarian, rigid, firm, with meaning suspended until it is disclosed at the end of the text. Since the events are fixed, meaning, which is suspended, is also fixed and only revealed at the end of the text. The major difference between deconstruction and the realist reading is that the classic realist is closed while deconstruction is open. But it will be deconstruction that will be our mode of operation in understanding the novel: *Their Eyes Were Watching God*.

The novel takes its title from a horrifying scene where the hurricane seemed to be tearing everything apart and the people in a room, rather than running away for shelter, were petrified and paralyzed with fear. The title- *Their Eyes Were Watching God* seems to be a misnomer since it presupposes that these people were deep in their prayers to God. They were not really praying. They were simply paralyzed with fear. The kind of fear that seems to intoxicate. And so the question is: why does the writer bring God into the action, when in fact the thrust of the action seems to point elsewhere! The answer lies in what Paul de Mann calls "The Grammatization of Rhetoric and the Rhetorization of Grammar." Grammar being a straight line is easily subverted by Rhetoric with its polymorphous perversities of voices. These plurality of voices are the voices of deconstruction that will be used to read the critical contention of this text as it deals with the theme of: "A Woman's Struggles to Exert an Identity and Exert Her Voice Through Her Marriages." The text will interrogate Janie Crawford's marriages to her first, second and third husbands and then attempt to answer the question: "Was she ever able to establish her identity and so find her own voice?"

Janie Crawford was born in hard times. Times when a woman's security and satisfactory well being depended on marrying a good man. Good, in the sense that he could provide food on the table. This is why all women with marriageable daughters depended on arranged marriages to store up their daughters safely:

> Taint Logan Killicks at wants you to have, baby, it's protection ah ain't gitting ole, honey. Ah'm done ole. One morning soon, now, de angel wid the swords is goin tuh stop by here. De day and hour is hid from me, but it won't be long. At ast de Lawd whom you was uh infant in mah arms to let me stay here till you got grown. He spared me to see the day. Mah daily prayer now is tu let dese golden moments roll on a few days longer till ah see you safe in life. (p. 30)

The persuasive solemnity of Nanny's sermon to her granddaughter brittles with sympathy, religious faith and contradiction. In her opening sentence, she is asking her to marry a man for protection. So, really, she is not asking her to marry him, but marry protection. This is the double nature of irony when an answer to a question is buried deep in the dark Labyrinth of the question and the question itself maybe the answer. In her sermon, Nanny does not mention love, one of the vital elements for a successful marriage. So, even though the silent movement of the narrative is towards protection, yet there seems to be some naturally built-in mechanism in this progression that is poised to subvert the craved protection. God had let her live to see her granddaughter grow up. But this same God did not command her to give the girl out to bondage. It is easy to see that the very intentions she had to get her married, will be the same reasons that will subvert her marriage, happiness or the longevity of that marriage. Also, something really serious is lacking in her request. Janie's voice, the voice of acceptance, the voice of consent is blatantly lacking. So, even though she discovered her identity in the picture with a white family, her voice was repressed with the white family, just as it was with her grandmother. And because she was not consulted, because love was not so important in the world view of her grandmother, that was one contributing factor to the easy collapse of her first marriage. This is why she took off with a stranger, Joe Starks, without even the courtesy of a divorce.

But this action, deliberate as it was, seems to be the first sign of Janie exerting her identity and even her voice. This is the first time she takes her life into her own hands and doing it her own way! That was why:

> Janie hurried out of the front gate and turned south. Even if Joe was not there waiting for her, the change was bound to do her good. (p. 54)

In a third person narrative, Hurston tells the story of a strong willed woman who was ready to go on her own to change her circumstances. This was a beautiful change from a life of command, obedience, servitude and subservience to freedom. This was her declaration of independence from the control not only by her husband, but from the community and societal grips as seen from the fact that she did not get a divorce and the decision to leave was quick and really decisive. Maybe she was so decisive because Logan Killicks was different from Joe Starks, her second husband.

If the life with Logan Killicks was that of drudgery, frustration, mental mutilation, doubt, hope and even desire, Joe Starks offered hope in flamboyance and wealth! But it was with Joe Starks, however, that the institution of marriage would receive its severest test. The test was to prove the equation that: "Man, wealth and an independent woman would equal a happy marriage!" In this relationship, would Janie trade her freedom for wealth? Or was freedom more important to keep than wealth? The second test was: "Would Joe Starks be able to keep his wife because of the sheer weight of his influence as a mayor and his wealth? Somebody or something must give!

Janie's life with Joe was that of sporadic happiness as well as frustration because she tended to protect her identity and freedom very precariously. It was a life of repressed anger which she carefully unleashed with method and calculation. Most critics of this novel, from Robert Stepto, to Alice Walker, entertain a funny speculation about Janie's inability to achieve her voice. The question of voice to me seems irrelevant to the contentions of the novel which are the maintenance of an identity and the freedom to keep that identity unblemished.

Janie always had her voice and knew when it was most effective to use it. And she used it very effectively if we trail her life with Joe Starks. In their husband and wife feuds that seemed to unveil their mutual anger, frustration, doubt, hope and even desire, we can listen to Janie's voice very clearly. The question that most critics have failed to ask is: "Can an independent free spirited woman be married?" The question is critical because marriage implies a surrender of divided loyalties for the good of the family. A woman who feels that she can be an island has no need for a man. Marriage implies surrendering certain freedoms for the sake of the greater good! Excessive individualism is simply antithetical to marriage! It is like the individual who refuses to pay tax and turns around to complain if he/she is denied public communal privileges. If we trail Janie's life as a shopkeeper and mayor's wife, the incident with the sick mule, the age furry, to her unholy war with her husband, even on his death bed, we realize that her eternal worries and contentions were on how to protect her identity and not about finding her voice.

As a mayor's wife and a shopkeeper of (the only shop in the city), she enjoyed a certain privilege that most women envied. She was a world of her own. She was also a class of her own. But these privileges come with a certain price. Since she was uneducated, she had to take instruction from her rich husband. This would have been an easy trade for an ordinary woman who would thank God for His amazing grace. But not with Janie. Janie could not take instructions particularly when they were not polite and somehow, sublimely sensitive! And Joe Starks on the other hand, saw no reason to apologize to a woman he has given everything. He knew more about business than his nagging wife! The world of business is brutal and only the strong succeed. And so, he pounded commands and reprimands when necessary! But, rather than learning from these instructions, Janie developed an anger that boiled and festered. Maybe some of her anger was directed at her lack of freedom to make decisions in a business she really did not fully understand. Fused with this anger, she immediately personalized the incident of the sick mule that was tied to a tree, teased and about to be killed. In her mind, she immediately saw the restrictions and the tease on the mule as a symbol of her life of restrictions, obedience, servitude and a haunting helplessness:

> A little war of defense for helpless things was going on inside her. People ought to have some regard for helpless things. But ah hates disagreement and confusion, so ah better not talk. It makes it hard to get along. She wanted to fight about it. (p. 57)

In this piece, we hear the voice of the omniscient writer reading the mind of her hero. A hero who has compassion for a poorly treated mule. The kind of treatment that would seem synonymous with the treatment Janie got at the hands of her husband. In a veiled defense of Janie, as seen from her remarks about the brutality to the mule, the writer also indicts the society, the community and even the world for our callousness towards the defenseless! But there is something native to language that seems to instigate a contradiction between the omniscient writer's intentions and the contradictions in that language. The main contradiction stems from the fact that the war cries of the author seem to be in direct conflict with that of her hero. The writer in this piece, shows the rebellious posture of Janie's mind, while in her own voice Janie seems only concerned with reconciliation, harmony and peace. It is at this point in the novel that it would appear the writer lost control of her hero because the writer and hero seem to be dancing to the tunes of different drummers.

It is of importance to note that while the writer in this piece seems obsessed with the problems of freedom and restrictions, Janie seems more inclined to compromise and harmony. It would seem like while the writer is more concerned with the problems of power and restrictions, Janie in her own voice appreciates the benefits of compromise which leads to peace and harmony! But this inclination towards compromise was tested when this husband and wife, engaged each other in a family feud before a crowd with their bragging rights on age.

The sensitivity of age to both people had been carefully relayed by the author. She narrates the awkward nature of Joe's physical appearance and the fact that even Janie was past forty. All the writer needed was an occasion that would explode this feud. The explosion occurred one day when Joe remarked that Janie was an old woman that nobody, no man would care for. The dialogue that ensued was sober but bitingly debilitating, particularly when it happened in front of Joe's friends:

T'aint no use getting all mad Janie, cause ah mention you ain't no young gal no mo! Nobody in heah ain't looking for no wife outa yah. Old as you is.

Jamie: "Naw, ah ain't no young gal no mo' but den ah ain't no old woman neither. Ah reckon ah looks mah age too. But I am a woman every inch of me, and ah know it. Dats a uh whole lot more'n you kin say. You bit-bellies round here and put out a lot of brag, but, 'taint nothing to it but you big voice. Humph! Talking about me looking old! When you pull down yo britches you look lak de change yu life." (p. 122)

This dialogue reveals the smoldering anatomy of the anger and frustration of the marriage and the disturbing vermin that it unleashed to break the love and marriage. The author, narrator, had prepared the reader through her narrative of the anger. The scene is clear cut. Joe would start by attacking Janie at her most vulnerable and sensitive spot: "Her marriageable worth and her age." The author relays Joe's attack as an effort to control by mentally tarnishing Janie's physical image, her mental composure and even tolerance. The idea is that every woman in Janie's position: rich, well placed and comfortable, would tolerate these attacks. But Janie was a different woman who fought back without tact, sensitivity or restraint. Any woman in Janie's position at this time in history would have withdrawn to the back and cried. Then confront her husband later in bed about his verbal cruelty. But Janie was not that kind of a woman. That was why her (Janie's) response was a calculated, well organized attack that shows no respect for her husband, nor his friends who sat with him. And so she braced for an onslaught.

First, she defends her self image in contradicting terms, claiming that she may not be a young girl, but she was certainly not an old woman. The contradiction is that you can not have it both ways. You are either old or young. And she attempts to reinforce her age by claiming that she looks her age! What age? Is this the young age or the old? She then unleashes her most destructive weapon when she claimed that she is every inch a woman unlike Joe. Here, the implication is that perhaps Joe's virile sexual organ was dead. He maybe impotent because he shows all signs of diabetes and overweight! For the sake of socially accepted decorum, Janie could have stopped her onslaught here. But she over killed when she started pointing at her husband's disgusting anatomy. To make it more cruel and even bizarre, she was attacking him before his friends. Not only did she dethrone Joe physically and emotionally, she attacked Joe's power and his helplessness in the hands of his own wife. A situation that every man usually dreads! At this point in the narrative, the question of Janie's voice would look ridiculously irrelevant. It was to protect her feminine identity that she fought so furiously. It was not to find her voice. She already had one. A voice with a sharp edge like a razor.

It was with this voice that she unleashed her severest attacks on her husband even on his deathbed when all he needed was love and compassion. But Janie saw her husband's illness as an opportunity to lash him with his own vermin:

> Janie: "Naw, Jody, it wasn't because ah don't have no sympathy. Ah had uh lavish uh dat. Ah just didn't never git no chance tuh use none of it. You wouldn't let me."
>
> Jody: "Dat's right, blame everything on me. Ah wouldn't let you show no feelings! When Janie dats all ah ever wanted or desired. Now, you come blaming me." (p. 85)

This last speech, an intrusion into the life of a man dying was, I think, the most savage blow that Janie ever landed her husband. The poignant and revolting part of it was that she brutalized him verbally at a time he needed her love and compassion and when he was weakest. Her excuse was that she never had any opportunity to show her soft feelings. But the irony was that the opportunity was right there, at Jody's deathbed and she was too selfish to see it. Perhaps the most cruel thing she did was to tease him with the inevitability of his death. This was awful because even death does not want to know of itself.

The author's sympathy at this point, seems to swing to Jody. This is because she shows Janie's true personality as uncaring, selfish, self-absorbed hound who seemed more concerned about her remaining scrappy beauty. It may seem cruel or extreme to suggest that Janie drove her husband to a quick death after that bitter speech and then turned around to rejoice after his death. At this point, it would look ridiculous to even suggest that Janie did not have her voice, nor that she was struggling to have her voice. She had it. But then used it sparingly and even savagely. It was her identity, her femininity buried in her appearance that she fought to protect and she had no trouble flaunting it when she found the opportunity.

There is a universal axiom that sometimes people love three times before they meet real love. Janie had this opportunity for self-realization with her third husband, Tea Cake! With Tea Cake, the economic dynamics changed hands. This is because in her previous marriages, she was hooked to a man because of his wealth. But with Tea Cake, the woman and not the man had the money. Tea Cake, the writer tells us so warmly, was the best of Janie's husbands because he respected her as a woman and a good human being. Tea Cake was also spontaneous, active, saw and wanted all the joys of life for him and his wife. She rewards his kindness very warmly in:

> Once upon uh time, ah never expected nothing, Tea Cake, but being dead from standing still and trying tuh laugh. But now you come along and made something outa me. So ah'm thankful fuh anything we come through together. (p. 167)

This piece shows a warm satisfaction in marriage. Something her former husbands could not provide. Her former husbands created nothing but boredom and unhappiness. Tea Cake brought out her real self. He made her reach her self-actualization. This is because he created a life of mutual respect, trust and love. A perfect match. But this marriage made from heaven was tested at a critical point: "The point was to choose whose life should be sacrificed to live or die." Janie selected her own life. She shot and killed her own husband, Tea Cake, even though under very auspicious circumstances. And in killing Tea Cake, she fulfilled her own prophecy that there are two things that are unavoidable, one is to go to God and to find out how to live for oneself. By killing Tea Cake, Janie had consolidated her life and identity. She had nothing left to defend and that was why she was silent in her own trial. She ran a good race. A race she knew she would win.

The theory of deconstruction focuses on contradictions in a text and the plurality of voices. The contradiction in this text is seen in the subvertion of the Grammar of the text by Rhetoric, language. The Grammar of this theme was the brutality of Black men at this point in history to their wives. But language (Rhetoric) subverts this theme because at the end of the novel, language reveals that in fact it is the woman who seems to have that awful heart of darkness and not the man. And so, the beauty of this text is in the muted site of pleasure and bliss in the rhetoric because: it granulates, it crackles, it caresses, it grates, it cuts, it comes: that is bliss. (Barthes. The Pleasure of the Text, p. 67)

Chapter 7

To Criticize the Critics of Zora Neale Hurston's: *Their Eyes Were Watching God*

> The art inspired by God's laughter does not by nature serve ideological certitudes, it contradicts them. Like Penelope, it undoes each night the tapestry that the theologians, philosophies and learned men have woven the day before."
> Milan Kundera. *The Art of the Novel*, p. 160.

Literature from it's earliest inception has suffered the frustrating bouts of anxieties, frustrations, hopes, doubts and even desires of the problems related to inclusion/exclusion, commitment/non-commitance. These anxieties date back as early as the age of Saint Augustine, who Adrian Marino claims paraphrased Psalm LXX to mean: He who is not acquainted with the letters (Litteratura Grammatica) will not be admitted into the kingdom of God (Bio. Of Lit., p. 44). And Saint Abelard who claimed that: It is better to be a Grammarian than a Heretic (Ibid. p. 44). If we listen to the silent voices of the church fathers, we will sense that concern for separation and commitment. And the choices are grim and dizzy for the simple fact that for Augustine all the Pagans and uneducated were excluded from the Kingdom of God. The overwhelming implication, however, is that even God, Himself, was on the side of Literature. The ugly nausea here is that God would not reward you for your faith and good works, but for your intellectual achievements which are really man made. As for Saint Abelard, the Heretic and the grammarian were on two very irreconcilable fences. But God, in the same case, is on the side of the grammarian, the man of letters. The disturbing twist here would be the case of one who is a Heretic and a grammarian or a grammarian who happens to be a heretic! Where would they go? This ugly dichotomy between the literature of commitment and non commitance, according to Marino, reached its highest frenzy, its penacle, during the renaissance and humanist enlightenment where Etienne Dolet was burned at the stakes as a "victim of this grim (Catholic Churches) totalitarian mentality." The focal point of the criticism of Zora Neale Hurston's writing, particularly her novel: *Their Eyes Were Watching God*, was on this contention between commitment and non-commitance, submission/resistance.

However, before we criticize the critics of Hurston's novel, we must make an attempt at understanding the meaning of the word: Literature. But this attempt is simply that, an attempt, a shot in the dark because the word is as elusive as the wind. That is why nobody seems to agree to the real meaning of Literature. Literature for Jean Paul Sartre, in his text (*What is Literature?*) is a text that aims at exposing the social anomalies of a society and by so doing, change them. This kind of Literature is committed. This Literature is committed to naming the evils of society. And by naming, we change the mythical and mysterious aura of the thing named. By naming, we change the thing so named.

This kind of Literature is calculated to change the course of history. But Theodor Adorno claims that since man did not invent history, how can he change it? Literature for Terry Eagleton is a social and political decision made by a few who hope to reward or condemn a particular text for the sole aim of control and power. But the best attempt at defining Literature comes from a tediously turgid, intellectual text written by Adrian Marino: *The Biography of the Idea of Literature*.

The notion of a biography as against the notion of the history of Literature may have some warm implications. Some of these implications stem from the word Biography because it has some human flavor to it because it deals with the history of an individual's life as it pertains to his/her anxieties, frustrations, hopes, doubts and even desires. Literature, like the human being enjoys some of these symptoms. But history, on the other hand, could mean: time, chronology, sequence, progression, contiguity, continuity and even cause and effects. This sense of history, however, refers to the old traditional notion of history. The new reading of history is that history does not solely mean chronology and sequence. History today could come from an accident, sporadic and even mysterious. History could happen out of omission or divine intervention like that mysterious light on Pentecost Sunday! So, Dr. Marino's book: *The Biography of the Idea of Literature*, because it catches that very warm essence of the narrative of human consciousness, seems to me to be the best definition of the word: Literature.

At this point, let me mention only two novels of the 18th century that have universal acceptance into the canon as Literature. These novels are Flaubert's: *Emma Bovary* and Lawrence Sterne's: *Tristram Shandy*. According to Milan Kundera, in his, *The Art of Fiction*, Flaubert invented stupidity in *Emma Bovary*. Emma's stupidity stems from the fact that she wades from one error to another as if in a trance even to her deathbed. And her male accomplices watch her patiently like petrified ghosts in a funeral oration. Kundera claims that this stupidity does not go away with the advent of progress and even technology. This stupidity cruises along side by side with progress! Lawrence Sterne, on the other hand saw the efficacy in the use of digression. So, when he collapsed cause and effects in *Tristram Shandy*, Sterne created a language that was pure and quintessential and so he moved language directly to God. *And Vox populi, Vox dei*.

As we have labored, a labor of love, to understand the meaning, implications and complications, denotations/connotations of the word Literature, we will now attempt to discuss the critics of Zora Neale Hurston, particularly those who scrutinized her novel: *Their Eyes Were Watching God*.

The notion of marginalization has some painful implications for a writer, particularly if this was incurred out of no significant fault of the writer. This writer's fate becomes similar to that poor child who grows up in a very rich neighborhood. This child will certainly be scourged by "The Slings and Arrows of Outrageous Fortune." Maybe he/she will learn from it and become stronger. Or he/she maybe simply overwhelmed and therefore crushed. Zora Hurston, because of her indomitable spirit to resist the prevailing Literature of commitment, of mainstream voices, of merciless black male abrasion, suffered a deliberate or inadvertent omission from extensive literary study. That is why an incursion into the study of her works appears like the search for that deliberate history of neglect where the past and present are muted in that narrative voice of the telling! This text is a joyful study of the critical comments of scholars who found it safe to study and scrutinize Hurston's works, particularly her novel: *Their Eyes Were Watching God*. Some of the scholars in this study include: Henry Louis Gates (Jr.), Mae Gwendolyn Henderson, William Andrews, Alice Walker and Robert Hemenway.

Professor Gates in his: *Zora Neal Hurston: A Negro Way of Saying*, praises the wealth of her autonomous imagination, the lyrical nostalgia of the novel and the compounding complicity of Janie Crawford's marriages in:

> The chastity of Janie Crawford's fulfillment as an autonomous imagination, *Their Eyes* is a lyrical novel that correlates the need of her first two husbands for ownership of progressively larger physical space (and the gaudy accoutrements of upward mobility) with the suppression of self-awareness in their wife. Only with her last lover, a roustabout called Tea Cake whose unstructured frolics center around and about Florida swamps, does Janie at last bloom as does the large pear tree that stands beside her grandmother's tiny log cabin. (p. 287).

In this passage, Gates shows a warm and compassionate reading of this novel as he touches on the lyrical nostalgia, the autonomous imagination and the animal possessiveness of Janie's first two husbands. But my concern is that Gates seems to imply that upward mobility, the search for wealth, was the ugly ingredient that broke the two marriages. In simple language, it was the men's fault that their marriages collapsed. The contradiction in this line of thinking is that what Gates termed (autonomous imagination) another name for (individualism) is completely antithetical to a harmonious marriage. This judgement is based on the fact that marriage implies the surrender of divided loyalties for the benefit of the greater good. A woman who claims to be an island (individualism) has no need for a man.

Gates, however, with his intellectual wisdom is able to see and correlate the beauty, the joy, jouissance of a happy marriage with the passionate sexual rituals of a bee and the flowers in a pear tree:

> She saw the dust bearing bee sink into the sanctum of a bloom; the thousand sister calyxes arch to meet the love embrace and the ecstatic shiver of the tree from root to tiniest branch creaming in every bloom and frothing with delight. So, this was marriage. (p. 287).

Here we witness the nervous, dizzy, encounter with the bee and the blooms accelerating almost into orgasmic proportions. We can almost see the bee in our mind's eye sinking in and out of the blooms, igniting an orgasmic shiver that seems to rattle both the bee and the flower. Language here appears as if words were made flesh and seem to live amongst us. In this passage, the sensual beauty of Hurston's language, her delirious sensuality flows through those sexual insinuations in "the dust bearing bee sinking into the sanctum of the bloom;" a flirtation with the "thousand sister calyxes" that arch to meet the love embrace and the ecstatic shiver of the tree," which sends ripples of excitement to the tiniest branch creaming in every blossom and frothing with delight." These teeming sexual insinuations ignite a reader's five human senses that drag him/her along these visible and invisible cravings reminiscent of a warm passionate embrace of a first honeymoon. The sentences are pornographic and yet so pure that they could serve as models of English syntax. This is a paradise of language that is consummate with the explosive synthesis of the natural and the human sensibilities. However, for Professor Gates, Hurston's novel makes a social and aesthetic comment, for Mae Gwendolyn Henderson, the novel evokes a polymorphous perversity of language that has multiple denotations/connotations, diversities/congruities, implications/complications for a woman's labyrinth of repressive agencies.

The title of Henderson's text: *Speaking in Tongues,* evokes this aura, these vibrations, nuances of voices that appeal to the mystical, mythical, spiritual, human, the friend/enemy, the white man/white woman, the black man/black woman, all of whom directly or inadvertently put a black woman on trial each time she decides to write or speak. That title also ignites the different layers of responsibilities of a black woman who must serve and obey different masters. I will quote Henderson's whole passage here because of it's teeming rich insinuations:

> The challenge of Hurston's character is that of the Black woman writer—to speak at once to a diverse audience about her experience in a racist and sexist society where to be black and female is to be, so to speak, "on trial." Janie not only speaks in a discourse of gender and racial difference to the white male judge and jurors, but also in a discourse of gender difference (and racial identity) to the Black male spectators and a discourse of racial difference (and gender identity) to white women spectators. Significantly, it is the white male who constitute both judge and jury, and, by virtue of their control of power and discourse, possess the authority of life and death over the Black woman. In contrast, the Black man (who are convinced that the nigger (woman) kin kill . . . just as many niggers as she pleas) and white woman (who didn't seem

too mad) read and witness, oppose a situation over which they exercise neither power nor discourse. (p. 225-280).

The beauty of this passage is that it evokes multiple vibrations, layers, nuances of the repressive forces that confront a black woman each time she writes. A black woman confronts a hostile audience composed of gender/racial difference, white male (judge/jury) the black male (powerless but hostile) and the white woman (indifferent) but curious. It is in the spirit of these contentions that the metaphor of speaking in tongues becomes so captivating and authentic because it evokes the black and female writer's prowess. That title is captivating because it produces not only shock, but mystery in communication between man and man and between God and man. Interestingly, Henderson is also speaking in tongues through simulation and the shere drama of the mystery of the logic of her title. The mystery of speaking in tongues is that through the Holy Spirit, strange languages are heard and understood by a diverse group of people in their own traditional grounds, meanings and context. The only being who understands these multiple languages is God , Almighty. For the leity, this language serves only as a form of edification. And this brings us to the critical question for the black and female writer. That critical question for her is: How does she write so that her text will appeal to these multifarious and hostile groups? For her to succeed, will she require the power of the Holy Spirit, God Himself?

However, willingly or unwillingly (in the interest of survival) the black and female writer must write even though against her will and conscience to appeal to a white male audience, who like God, possess the power of physical and economic death. She must love herself enough and paradoxically hate herself enough to dance at once to the tune of different drummers. The white oppressor and the weak black male! These are critical choices that could make or break a black and female writer! The beauty of Henderson's text is that it captures that aura of the symbolic and the human, the thought and the utterance that appear so beautifully to be interchangeable. This is the text of bliss that Roland Barthes in his, *The Pleasure of the Text*, categorizes as:

> Text of Bliss: The text that imposes a state of loss, the text that discomforts (perhaps to a point of a concern for boredom) unsettles the reader's historical, cultural, psychological assumptions, the consistency of his tastes, values, memories, brings to a crisis his relation with language. (p. 14).

Barthes, in his warmness, captures those multiple auras of complications and complicity of language, style and delivery. These complications and complicity in language, style and delivery are what Henderson uses to evoke the multifarious, polymorphous perversities of a black and female writer's attempt to reach a diverse and often hostile audience.

However, if Henderson saw a black and female writer's style to involve speaking in tongues, for Alice Walker, Hurston and particularly her character Janie Crawford, are living female idols worthy of emulation. Ms. Walker in her essay: *Zora Neale Hurston, a Literary Biography*, remarked very candidly that if:

> Condemned to a deserted island for life, with an allotment of ten (10) books to see me through, I would choose, unhesitatingly two of Zora's novels: *Mules and Men* because I would need to be able to pass on to younger generations the life of American Blacks as legend and myth, and *Their Eyes Were Watching God* because I would want to enjoy myself while identifying with the black heroine, Janie Crawford, as she acted out many roles in a variety of settings and functioned (with spectacular results) in romantic and sensual love. There is no book more important to me than this one. (p. xiii).

Alice Walker raises Zora Neale Hurston's life and even the character in the novel, to the level of myth and legend worthy of emulation by the flowering generation of younger black women. But her remarks that the character, Janie Crawford "functioned with spectacular results in romantic and sensual love," is purely subjective and speculative depending on what side of the fence from which you observe Janie Crawford. And also depending on your frustrations, anxieties, hopes and even desires as they pertain to your gender. However, if Alice Walker saw Zora and her novels in terms of myth and legend, Karla Kaplan in her: *Zora Neale Hurston: A Life of Letters*, was concerned with Hurston's mastery of the black dialect.

Kaplan's recognition of the importance of the black dialect is worthy of note. This is because the black dialect is a domestication of English ("a language still comfortable in its ancestral home") but evoked to serve the peculiar needs of the moment. Kaplan remarked that:

> *Their Eyes Were Watching God*, Hurston's best novel, creates a character for whom the older human longing is self realization, but who offers her story to only one person—her best friend, Peoby. "Mouth

Almighty," as she calls the townspeople, "can't possibly understand. Ah ain't putting it in de street, Ah'm telling you." (p. 24)

In this short passage, Kaplan touches on Janie Crawford's eternal cravings, anxieties, frustrations, hopes and desires as they pertain to her self realization. And how Janie, obsessed with self realization, confronted the divided loyalties of individual and communal obligations and responsibilities. Kaplan touched again on how Janie tackled the problems of community gossips. A community whose role (like the Greek Chorus) becomes the judge and jury of individual and communal behavior. Silently, Kaplan hints at the effectiveness and the efficacy of the use of the black dialect. A language, that because of its proximity to the culture and history of a people, becomes the human and symbolic, authentic history of the past in the present. The beauty of the black dialect is because of these other bouncing advantages. One of the advantages is that, as a language forged through a history of anxiety and frustration, it always evokes individual and communal closeness in an utterance. But more important and poignant is the fact that dialect serves as escape and sanctuary from the master's voice! It should be of interest to note that Hurston (erroneously marginalized) did more for Harlem Renaissance than most other belligerent male writers. Her greatest contribution was that she alone may have seen the critical areas of contention, the battle field which was in: Language. The failure of the leaders of this movement (like those of Negritude in the 60's) to see the important role that language plays in a movement may have led to the collapse of that movement. Paul Jean Sartre shared his wisdom for the weakness of Negritude movement, which I think has an ancestral correlation with Harlem Renaissance.

Sartre reveals this painful logic in his "Black Orpheus," the role that language plays in the revolutionary movement of the colonized:

> The colonist has arranged to be the eternal mediator between the colonized; he is there—always there—even when he is absent, even in the most secret meetings. And since words are ideas, when the Negro declares in French that he rejects French culture, he accepts with one hand what he rejects with the other; he sets up the enemy's thinking-apparatus in himself like a crusher (p. 301)

Sartre captures in this piece, the emblem and problematics when the colonized rebels with the master's voice and language. This wisdom applies also to the contentions of Harlem Renaissance and Zora Hurston was the only candidate who wanted to start things right by deliberately developing the Black dialect. But rather than praise, she was marginalized. The modern reader of Black American Literature, particularly the writings of Zora Neale Hurston, must forgive the errors of the ancestors because the beauty of serendipity according to Umberto Eco is that:

> A number of ideas that today we consider false actually changed the world and how in the best instances, false beliefs and discoveries totally without credibility could lead to the discovery of something true. (p. 111).

So, Hurston maybe the only writer that history has rewarded very richly, but only out of omission. This notion of literary omission, a lack of knowledge of facts and content, appears so blatantly in a remark by William Andrews on the artistic quality of Hurston's art.

William Andrews in *Classic Fiction of Harlem Renaissance* remarked that,

> After World War II, the increasing conservative case of her writing (Zora) which was invested much more in Journalism than fiction led to Hurston's almost total eclipse as a literary figure in the 1950's. (p. 77)

Here is a statement almost bordering on criminal negligence for the lack of knowledge or understanding of Zora Hurston's outstanding qualities as a literary artist. The nauseating aura of Andrew's remark hovers around the words: Conservative and Journalism. My concern for the use of the word conservative to categorize Hurston's art is that the term is vague, with no aesthetic logic except to reinforce a marginalization similar to what Saint Abelard remarked about Grammarians and Heretics: "It is better to be a Grammarian than a Heretic." But while the beauty in Abelard was that God Himself was on the side of the Grammarian, Conservatism on the other hand is vaguely used to denote political affiliation: The opposite of liberalism! And nobody who has read *Their Eyes Were Watching God* would, in good conscience, classify Hurston as a journalist. A perjured term that signifies writing as plain, predictable, transparent and plastic.

Valerie Smith has a different point of view than Andrews. Valerie Smith in: *Black Feminist Theory* comments on Dianne Sadoff's revelation of the problematic of Hurston's portrayal of her character and Alice

Walker's ambivalent stances on gender and biological motherhood. She claims:

> Sadoff's examination of the relationship between Zora Neale Hurston and Alice Walker reveals a compelling tension between the explicit subject of each author's work and the subversive material that underlies those surfaces. An ancestor claimed as significant by most recent black women writers, *Zora misrepresents herself* with her fiction. Sadoff claims *Their Eyes* . . . may announce itself, for instance as a celebration of heterosexual love, but Hurston manipulates narrative strategies to ensure that the male is eliminated and the female liberated. Sodoff goes on to show that Walker affirms her tie to Hurston by inscribing a similar double agenda throughout her work, problematizing the status of heterosexual love in similar ways. Moreover, while her essays document her enthusiastic pursuit of Hurston as a literary foremother, her novels display a profound anxiety about biological motherhood. Sadoff's reading demonstrates, then, that the peril of uniqueness compels an intense need on the part of black women writers to identify a literary matrilineage even as their historical circumstances occasion their ambivalence about the fact and process of mothering. (p. 377).

Smith's essay celebrates the politics of gender and sexual persuasions with regards the works of Alice Walker and Zora Neale Hurston. So, of course, it is the enunciating, an exposé of the comments that Dianne Sodoff made with regards to the duplicity and subversion lurking in the work of Alice Walker and Hurston. According Smith, Sodoff takes issues with Hurston's seeming celebration of heterosexuality while on the hand, through narrative strategy, she kills a husband to free the woman in the novel. This is a misrepresentation of herself because the character of Janie Crawford originally was demonstrating the uncaring, repressive and savage behavior of men towards women. But when the bell rings at the end of the novel, instead of the man, it is the woman, in fact, who has that disturbing heart of ugly darkness. But the funny thing about Sodoff's comment is that she did not listen to Janie Crawford's greedy selfish, self seeking maxims of life which were: "Two things everybody's got th do fuh theyselves. They got th go th God, and they got to find out about livin fuh theyselves." (p. 192). These two maxims were a sad commentary and demonstration of Janie Crawford's attitude to life. She knew that death was inevitable. But her primary duty in life was to take care of herself and the world could go to blazes. So, yes,

Sodoff may be right that Hurston misrepresented not only herself but all women and men who have faith in the institution of marriage. And some who are ready to put their lives on the line to protect each other. Not every woman will pick up a gun and kill a husband who has a mental problem! Alice Walker's dilemma is in the difficult problem of straddling the fence between heterosexuality and lesbianism. That is why her essays and novels seem to dance to the tunes of two different drummers. Valerie Smith's concern seems to hover around the problems of choosing literary ancestors based mainly on artistic quality rather than sexual and gender persuasions. In other words: which is more important to affiliate with: A high artistic quality and production or gender and sexual persuasion? Or can one separate one from the other and still do justice to both collectively or individually? These are difficult questions.

However, my concern is: what does the politics of sex and gender have to do with the quality of artistic creation? Should literary discussion not focus on the creative talent of Hurston as seen from the delicious deliriousness of her syntax, the pornographic enchantment of her sentences or the juicy lyrical nostalgia of her words! The sense of sadness and joy, of boredom and excitement and the loaded philosophic propensity of her characters are what make Hurston so joyful to read.

The intrusion of this politics of gender and sex into the artistic quality of a writer is not restricted only to Hurston. Joan Acocella in her book: *Willa Cather and the Politics of Criticism*, complains about the way that Willa Cather's artistic work has been vilified by excessive political erudition and so wonders:

> Should politics be left out of literary criticism? How can it be? It is part of the critic's intellectual world. If it is not there explicitly, it will be there implicitly, as today's political critics have repeatedly pointed out. The problem with these critics writings, however, is not that they contain politics, but that they contain almost nothing else. (p. 66).

Ms. Acocella posed very rich but disturbing questions about the trend of modern critical practice, where most critics focus only on the politics of a text to the exclusion of the literary artistic merit. T.S. Eliot in anticipation of the verdict on D.H. Lawrence's *Lady Chatterley's Lover*, warned in his book: To criticize the critic, the intellectual changes to a text when a critic restricts his/her judgement of a text mainly to its moral or (political) quality, while excluding the intellectual and the artistic:

> My particular reason for referring to my response to the work of Lawrence is that it is well to remind ourselves, in discussing the subject of literary criticism, that we can not escape personal bias, and that there are other standards besides that of literary merit which can not be excluded. It was noticeable in the Chatterley case, that some witness for the defense defended the book for the moral intensions of the author rather on the ground of its being important as a work of literature. (p. 25).

Eliot, in this piece, is referring to that ridiculous inquisition where D.H. Lawrence's novel: *Lady Chatterley's Lover* was taken to the court of law to be tried for its excessive moral promiscuity. Eliot in this case shares the same concerns with Ms. Acocella as it pertains to the role of the critic. Eliot agrees that though a critic can not escape his personal bias which could be political, philosophical, psychological, moral or even spiritual, that critic should also be cognizant of the literary and intellectual. The errors that the persecutors made in this case of *Chatterley* in restricting criticism solely to the moral intentions of the author, are the same errors that critics of Willa Cather and Zora made in seeing only the gender and sexual persuasions of these writers. The literary call then is for a critic to try to balance the political and the literary merit as part of his/her literary judgement. But, my concern is: Is this possible? Is it possible to synthesize the political and the literary (a kind of mutation!) without doing damage to the individual or the collective judgement. And what about the ominous implications of Kenneth Burke's alchemy. Kenneth Burke in his: *A Grammar of Motives*, claims that when two different elements are combined in a chemical reaction, they produce an alchemy (a compound) that is completely different from the elements that formed it.

So, in this case of combining, balancing the political with the literary, will a new compound be formed that will neither be of moral or literary merit? What will we have? What comes out of this alchemy is: The Death of Literary Criticism! There are however, some critics of Zora's novel who focused mainly on the novel's artistic quality. Some of these writers include: George Stevens, Larry Neal and Sterling Brown.

George Stevens in his essay *Negroes by Themselves*, points out the technical weakness as well as the artistic enunciation of Negro dialect in the novel, claiming that:

> The only weak spots in the novel are technical; it begins awkwardly with a confusion and unnecessary preview of the end; and the dramatic action, as in the story of the hurricane, is sometimes clumsily handled. Otherwise the narration is exactly right because most of it is in dialogue, and the dialogue gives us a constant sense of character in action. No one has ever reported the speech of Negroes with a more accurate ear for its raciness, its rich invention, and its rich music. (p. 237).

The technical problems that Stevens remarked about maybe accurate. But in this instance, Hurston may have been practicing with James Joyce's, Stream of Consciousness where in (Marion Bloom) in Ulysses, Joyce tries to capture the dream of the flirting human self so that we could watch it for a minute. And Stevens comments on the artistic accuracy of the black dialect with its musical nostalgia are quite on the mark as I have commented earlier.

However, Larry Neal in his essay: *Eatonville's Zora Neale Hurston: A Profile*, concentrates on the Blues aesthetic of the novel. But being ignorant of the quality of the content of good Blues music, I will offer only a flimsy and layman's comment. The difference, to me, between Blues music and Country Western is that while Country music celebrates love, deception and the hope of reconciliation, Blues music seems to celebrate the painful experiences of a history of a people, such as their anxieties, frustrations, doubts, hopes and even desires. And all these symptoms are muted into an agonized history of suffering, scourge and stigmatization.

In conclusion, this text has been an attempt to deal with the anxieties, frustrations, hopes and even desires that were inflicted on Zora Neal Hurston's novel: *Their Eyes Were Watching God*. And we know that though beaten, she was not bowed, as we listen to her defiant remark in: What it means to be colored me:

> I am not tragically colored. There is no great sorrow damned up in my soul, nor lurking behind my eyes—no one on earth had a greater chance for glory. (p. 77).

The universal maxim that "You cannot keep a good person down" may be true in this case.

Chapter 8

Dialect as Art in *Their Eyes Were Watching God*

The word "art" provokes immediately in our consciousness a feeling about such great works as Michelangelo's painting of the Cistern Chapel, or those gothic mediaeval figures that we see in great Cathedrals in Venice, Tuscany or Milan. But in terms of dialect, that is not the kind of art that we are thinking about. We are here thinking about language as art that communicates meaning, pleasure, craves a communal closeness (an association, historical and earthy). Something that is therapeutic to a point of a catharsis. We are thinking of dialect as art. Art that is a double and yet real, a mimesis that yet craves the original. Language as an art that craves and at the same time mocks that craving even in its very authenticity. We are thinking of dialect as art. The same kind of art that seems to have the kind of nuances that Albert Camus thought about in his: *Art as a Communion*:

> Must art therefore be divine?
>
> No. But art is a means of arriving at the divine some might reproach us for lowering art, by considering it a means. But means are sometimes more beautiful than truth. Who has not dreamed of a book or a work of art that would be only a hopeful beginning, profoundly unfinished? There are other means as well besides art: They are called faith and love. (p. 221)

When we take a sober meditation at the meaning and content of the above passage, we will be amazed at the richness of its content and the deliciousness of its significations. So, we must be careful and really hesitant in answering the question: "muse art therefore be divine?" That question is coded and even loaded with different connotations/denotations of various schools of art and their overall assumptions. Some schools, which date back to antiquity (and ancients) believed art to be divine. That was why the early church worshiped pictures of Christ and Saints.

Pictures (art) were a means to spread the faith by the early church to the uneducated. Even in today's Africa, some tribes still pay homage to their (idols) art. But this form of devotion is really transcendental because it moves from the art (the object) to the supreme deity. So, the answer is a (yes/no). Art should be art, but also transcendental. Camus believes that the (means) is sometimes more enjoyable than the truth. The means here implies how human beings handle their anxieties, frustrations, mutilations, doubts, hopes and even desires. He also seems to suggest that in the journey of life, the middle passage, the struggles of the passage and even the frustrations with all the composite anchors of these human activities are sometimes more enjoyable than the end of the journey.

This is where I sometimes quarrel with some of Saint Paul's utterances like: "I run a race that I know I will win." My concern here is: how does he know? Is he God? Is he playing God to himself? How can God know God? Secondly, in the game of life, is winning everything? What about enjoying the trauma or treat of that journey. What about that sophistic warning by the Lord Jesus when he said that those who keep their life will lose it and those who lose it will keep it! We may all prefer the trauma or treat of that middle passage that Camus is concerned with! And this brings us to the crucial question of dialect as art in Hurston's novel: *Their Eyes Were Watching God*.

By listening to the contentions of Camus about art, dialect in this novel is a form of art that comes near the divine. This dialect however is not really divine, but a means of communication with the divine. An art that relays information with joy, bliss, jouissance and all the quintessential human cravings. We are thinking of dialect as art, that is even sometimes therapeutic to the point of a catharsis. Hurston's art is sometimes language as a double, a mimesis that yet craves the original and sometimes even mocks that craving even in its very authenticity. So, we come face to face with a dialect that comes very close to the divine when we hear Nanny, trying to plant a moral seed in a young girl's mind the first time this girl steals a kiss. A girl, at an age when sex seems more delicious than morality:

> "Look at me, Janie don't set dere
> wid you head hung down.
> Look at yo ole grandma!"
> Her voice began snagging on the
> prongs of her feelings. "Ah
> don't want to be talking to yo
> lak dis. Fact is ah done been
> on mah knees to mah Maker
> many's de time askin'
> please—for Him not to make
> de burden too heavy for me to
> bear" (p. 13)

This passage dramatizes dialect as an art form that comes very close to the divine. Dialect as art that communicates not only meaning, but meaning that absorbs power into itself and so, transfers this power from man to God. When Nanny reminds the girl to "Look at yo ole grandma," she provokes a feeling of pathos/ethos in a girl who sees her grandma not only as an authority figure, but an earthly representative of God in the family. But the most poignant nature of this speech is that it seems as if (Grandma) is not talking directly to the girl, but talking above her. She is talking above her, reminding her of her pleas to God not to make the burden any heavier. So, she invokes the power and authority of God on a girl in a speech that pricks at the conscience, just at the same time that it consoles. So, is this dialect, this art, in this passage divine? The answer is a (yes/no) because the dialect has its own teasing divinity. But it is a divinity that is transcendental because it moves meaning, communication and power slowly from man to God, Himself.

So, we can now move slowly to confront dialect as an art that communicates feelings, emotions, anxieties, hopes, doubts and desires. We see dialect here as art that is therapeutic to a point of a catharsis. We encounter this feeling in a discussion between Janie and her Grandma on the efficacy of love in a marital relationship:

> If you don't want him, yo
> she oughta. Heah you is wid
> de on Liesch organ in town,

amongst colored folks in yo
parlor. Got a house bought
and paid for and sixty acres
Uh land right on the big
road and . . . awd have
mussy! Dats de very prong
all us black women gits
hung on. Dis love! Dat's
just what's got us uh
pullin and uh hauling
and sweating and doin'
from can't see in de mornin'
till can't see at night.
Dat's how come de ole folks
say dat be in uh fool
don't kill nobody. It jus
makes you sweat. Ah betcha
you wants some dressed
up dude dat got to look
at de sole of his shoes
everytime he cross de
street tut see whether he
got enough Leather dere
tut make it across.
You can buy and sell
such as dem wid what you got.
In fact you can buy 'em and give
'em away. (p. 23)

Here is dialect as art that, because of its historical context, could rightfully down-grade love, feeling, emotions when considering a marital union. Here is dialect as art that purges, cleanses, (therapeutic), a catharsis that comes (as it were) at the end of a grill, so that the reader and Janie are completely purged (off) any feeling or notion that love has anything to do with a happy marriage. Marriage, at the end of this passage, operates at pure capitalist economics of selling to the highest bidder. It makes a reader wonder if Tina Turner was really right in wondering: "What's Love Got To Do With It?" The effectiveness of this dialect, this art form, is because the message and meaning are coming from an old woman who (as it were) has gone through life's grill, so that her story is so very believable. Here is an art form, language as a flashback, so that the past and present are all muted in the present. Here is language and meaning that seem to clash, commenting and re-assessing each other. In this passage, this teeming emotional intensity in the mind of a grandmother, that she tries to cramp through the throat of her grand daughter is simply overwhelming. In her mind, marriage and love have lost their meaning. Their meaning is taken over by simple market economics, whose creed is to sell to the highest bidder. That is why an old man with a house and land (even though as old as dirt) is a better candidate for marriage than smooth, penniless Johnny! Love in this case becomes the culprit because it has: "got us pullin and uh hauling and sweating and doin' . . . from can't see in de mornin till can't see at night."

Perhaps, the beauty of this passage, this dialect is that it always unleashes a moral imperative. An imperative dressed in words deliciously enchanting because of the joy in the meaning and the lyrical music of the words. Secondly, the sense of detail that reinforces that moral imperative comes very close to John Ruskin's rich intellectual passion in dealing with gothic architecture and art. Marcel Proust in his book: *On Reading Ruskin*, restores to us this warm memory of John Ruskin as he rescued a minute Figurine in that sculpture of the Final Judgement at the tympana of that Gothic Cathedral of Saint Marks in Venice. The story is the same because real art resurrects, tells a story, fixes life in the eyes of eternity. And true art is moral. We must, therefore, because of the delicious sweetness of Proust and Ruskin's enchantment, listen fully to that voice of the master relaying the work of a master:

> At the call of Ruskin, we see the smallest figurine framing, a minuscule quatrefoil, resurrected in its proper form, looking at us with the same look that seems to be contained in but one millimeter of stone. No doubt poor little monster, I would not have been skilled enough, among the millions of stones of the cities, to find you, to make out your face, to rediscover your personality, to call you, to bring you back to life. But it is not that the infinity, that number, the nothingness which oppress us are very strong; it is that my imagination is not really strong. Indeed there was nothing truly beautiful in you. Your poor face, which I might never have noticed, does not have a very interesting expression, although evidently it has, like any person, an expression no one else ever had. But, since you lived enough to continue gazing with that same oblique glance for Ruskin to notice you and, after he had said your name, for his reader to be able to recognize you, are you living enough now, are you loved enough? (p. 47)

In this piece, we can almost listen to the voice of Proust in a humble, modest, endearing tribute to his hero. And even his attitude to the minuscule figurine is playful, gentle, patronizing but quintessentially enchanting in execution, particularly when his tribute to Ruskin turns to an address to the figurine in that playful, gentle and sweet delicacy that could send tremors to the soul of a reader. We see this gentle, almost fragile delicacy of appeal and patronage in: "No doubt poor little monster, I would not have been skilled enough among the millions of stones in the city to find you, to make out your face, to rediscover your personality, to call you, to bring you to life." This is an address to a small piece of stone in a building seen only through the eyes of a genius with all his gentle, delicate, sensibilities.

We watch with joy Proust's humility and modesty in: "it is that my imagination is not really strong," which really is an understatement because he could not have been sensitive and perceptive enough to have been looking for this figurine, and let alone find it without a strong imagination. And in an art (writing) that comes very close to the divine, Proust is able to absorb his respect for Ruskin into that beautiful power of his words as if to create an edifice worthy of human recognition, by elevating the power of Ruskin's work to that of God himself, the greatest Creator! We see this Ruskin's seeming divine power of creation in: "He said your name, for his reader to be able to recognize you."

Here is writing as simulation, as drama when Proust, like his hero, Ruskin, resurrects the figurine, gives it life in: "Are you living enough now, are you loved enough! Dear God! How can a stone answer?" It can not! But we, the spectators can register our gaze and lock that memory, that gaze in our soul for eternity, forever! I feel the same respect for Hurston's black dialect as Proust had for John Ruskin's art. This is because a reader can feel the same kind of sensibility that is sometimes mild/violent, playful/brutal depending on the context. One feels this same type of joy, of bliss muted with the tragic in Hurston's dialect.

A reader confronts this dialect as fun, the comic, joy and bliss muted with the tragic, when a gang of village gossipers gathered to laugh and mock Matt on the shape and demeanor of his mule:

Whuts wrong, Man: Ah ain't
after non uh y'alls foolishness
now.

Dat mule uh yourn, Matt. You better
go see 'bout him. He's bad off.

Matt: Where bout's. Did he wade in de
lake and uh allegator ketch him:

Walter: Worser'n dat. De women folks got
yo mule. When Ah come round the
lake 'bout noontime mah wife
and some others had him flat on de
ground using his sides fuh uh
wash board. (p. 52)

We witness here a gathering of the elite town gossipers , rain makers, the mouthpiece of the town, who like the Greek chorus become the judge and jury of communal and individual behavior. And the setting is a playful, relaxed Sunday morning when these gossipers have nothing else to do but talk trash! Today, this moment, the funny topic is that skinny Mule that belongs to Matt. The assumption of the group is that the mule is skinny because of lack of food, lack of care from its owner. This game, this hilarious tease starts when they see Matt coming to join them in a distance. The beauty, the joy of this passage resides in Matt's suspense, his gropping for answers, and absolutely at a breaking point before they reveal to him how a group of women have made his mule a wash board.

At this point, at this time of the disclosure that: "Mah wife and some others had him flat on de ground using his sides fuh uh wash board," the laughter, the cry, the comedy is at a breaking point! You have either to laugh, cry or be destroyed by the internal fuming of the comic. This is dialect as art that is comic. And a comedy that makes you laugh away all your worries, anxieties, frustrations and even hope! This is an art that is property of the community because it provokes communal closeness. A closeness that helps the community in the celebration of their rituals.

However, sometimes, this dialect as art, is used in the service of irony and sarcasm. And we know that irony and sarcasm usually split an argument, the symmetrical into bits and pieces. In the novel, Janie uses it quite frequently as a means of resentment, rebellion or simply to put up the other side of an argument. We see Janie's use of irony and sarcasm when she intrudes into a male discussion about a woman, Mrs. Robbins, who claims that her husband is negligent of parental responsibilities. He does not feed his family. Janie picks up this argument as a feminist defender of women's rights with subtle but tearing irony and sarcasm:

> Janie did what she had never done before, that is thrust herself into the conversation (male).
>
> "Sometimes God gits familiar wid us womenfolks too and talks His inside business. He told me how surprised He was 'bout y'all turning out so smart after Him making yuh different; and how surprised y'all is goin' tuh be if you ever find out you don't know half as much 'bout us as you think you do. It's so easy to make yo'-self out God almighty when you ain't got nothin' tuh strain against but women and chickens." (p. 75)

Hurston uses dialect here as art that uses irony and sarcasm to equal scores. Scores that deal with male arrogance pertaining to their claim of female ingratitude. In this carefully planned speech, Janie uses irony and sarcasm to attack the men in areas that they are most vulnerable such as their self depreciating arrogance of power and knowledge of women. She mocks the men under the deceptive cover of divine inspiration. In this instance, dialect, that art of speech is used as a weapon to fight back at men. A weapon of self defense that cuts deep into the seeming core of the problem: masculine arrogance and pride!

However, if Janie used dialect as irony and sarcasm to tear down men's pride, she used dialect also as art to declare freedom from history, freedom from parental control and the freedom to chart a course of life for herself. And this search for freedom through dialect, and dialect as an art comes to play in her decision to marry Tea Cake:

> Cause Tea Cake ain't Jody Starks
> and if he tried tuh be,
> it would be uh complete
> flommuck. But the minutes ah
> marries him everybody is goin' tuh
> be making comparisons.
> So us is goin off somewhere
> and start all over in Tea Cakes
> way. Dis ain't no business proposition
> and no race after property and titles.

> Dis is uh love game. Ah done
> lived Grandma's ways, now ah
> means tuh live mine. (p. 114)

Janie in this dialect behaves like St. Paul on his way to Damascus. She must have been struck by the wise, Holy Spirit of revelation that shows you the truth and it stays. Janie in this dialect knows that contrary to her Grandma's assumptions, love works better for a marriage than money, titles and property. She also significantly discovers that she must surrender her divided loyalties for the success of this union. She must surrender her life to her husband, rich or poor, but in the name of love. This becomes her theme that was completely contrary to her Grandma's teachings. It will appear as if living through the grill (Grandma's way) has taught her what works in a marriage. What works usually is not wealth but: Love! This is dialect as art. Art used in the service of truth! The beauty of Hurston's use of dialect is in the wisdom of selecting a medium (black dialect) instead of standard prose or poetry to present a metaphor that though individual, yet takes on a life that is universal. And this eclectic mooring of her mind is what Wole Soyinka, the Nigerian Nobel Prize winner in Literature in (1986) credits as essential qualities of the pure artistic mind. His remarks are found in his book: Art, Dialogue and Outrage:

> One of the tribulations of an eclectic approach to creativity which I consider the only reliable antidote to ever changing establishment monomania of the artistic world—is that genuine eclecticism manifests itself more in awareness than in appreciation. By that, I mean the eclectic mind employs for its own regulation a constant matrix of possible idioms of expression for a particular reality—be these idioms of history, politics, design, social change, eating, building, or sexual habits. From these various choices, it selects, evolves or recreates an apposite metaphor. (p. 44)

Soyinka in this piece shows us the wisdom of selective choices of idioms by an artist to serve her/his various needs. Hurston used dialect as art, as idiom in her enunciations of transcendental communication between man and the supreme being; dialect as art, as idiom, that portrays bliss, joy, jouissance and ecstasy. This dialect served her to represent language as mimesis, as therapy that moves towards a catharsis. Soyinka claims that it is this individualism of the artist that saves him/

her from the controlling strictures of institutional and even public stifling control and power. And we know that it was this mode of thinking that marginalized Hurston as an artist of substance in her era.

Soyinka's wisdom of the notion that "the eclectic mind employs for its own regulation a constant matrix of possible idioms of expression for a particular reality," played out over and over in this novel in the form of dialect as art, as idiom used in the service of love, of tenderness, and of passionate human sensibilities. We watch this tenderness on Tea Cake's deathbed when he fears that his wife may be flirting because he is too sick. We watch this mutual, passionate tenderness when Janie with humility accepts her old age, while Tea Cake, like a knight in shining armor, defends and protects the beauty and age of a waning flower:

> Janie: "Tea Cake, 'taint no use in bein' jealous uh me. In de first place ah couldn't love nobody but yuh. And in de second place, I just uh ole woman, dat nobidy want but yuh."
>
> Tea Cake: "Naw, you ain't neither. You only sould ole when you tell folks when wuz born, but wid de eys you'se young enough tuh suit most any man. Dat ain't no lie. Ah knows plenty mo' men would take yuh and work hard fuh de privilege. Ah done heard 'em talk." (p. 180)

This passage further confirms the beautiful utility of eclectic selectivity of idioms in the service of love. Dialect as art, as idiom, here, shows that love changes hearts and dissolves old boundaries. We see this change of heart in Janie's humble tenderness in playing down the issue of her age. We must remember that it was this age-quarrel that led her to almost drive a dagger through Joe Stark's heart. We also find a corresponding tenderness and masculine chivalry in Tea Cake's defense of his wife's age when it is so obvious that she was a waning flower. This is dialect as art, as idiom and language in the service of love. And with love all marriages are possible! This is eclecticism at its best, where language is used as an idiom, dialect and art in the service of an ideal, in the service of a philosophy of life and in the service of the sanctity of matrimony. And how that sanctity becomes a final solace, a sanctuary for a happy union between man and woman: marriage.

When life's journey has reached its end, its zenith, we gain experience through the turbulence or treat of that journey, that struggle in the middle passage which nobody can teach us except we pass through the grill ourselves. So, Janie at the end of her life, at the end of the rope, when she is confronted by her detractors who accuse her of murder and heartlessness, can through this language as art, as idiom, as dialect, calmly re-emphasize her credo, her philosophy of life, that guided her turbulent life in:

> Yo Papa and yo Mama and nobody else can't tell yuh and show yuh. Two things everybody got tuh do fuh themselves.
>
> They got tuh go tuh God, and they got tuh find out about livin' fuh themselves. (p. 192)

This passage is a classic demonstration of proving a case. *"Quod erat demonstradum."* Janie is the best candidate to show and prove that life's experience can not be taught. One has to go through the experience like going through a grill to understand life's sweetness and bitterness. She can at the end of her journey, claim like St. Paul: "I have run a good race. I have fought a good fight, or like McDonald in his unpublished sermon: I have given all. I have no more to give."

Epilogue

The Other Voice of Harlem Renaissance: Langston Hughes

Langston Hughes is a Negro poet, pure and simple. The word "Negro" has undergone transformations over the years, from "Colored" to "Black," and from Black to "African American." But the original meaning of the word derived from the descendants of Black slaves from Africa has not changed. This text will refer to that original native meaning. Langston Hughes, from beginning to end, treats only Negro themes. Some of the common Negro themes in his poetry are: the nostalgic craving for Africa; Racism; the Negro and Christianity; the problem of the Mulatto. But is being a Negro poet necessarily a negative comment on his poetry? I do not believe it is! I believe rather it should be a blessing because it provides a poet a fertile area of operation. Countee Cullen felt that Hughes emphasis on Negro themes narrowed his chances for recognition as a great poet, "Taken as a group the selections in this book are one sided. They tend to hurl the poet into a gaping pit that lies before the Negro writers, in the confines of which they claim racial artists instead of artists, pure and simple." (p. 39)

    I have my reservations about Cullen's remarks. I do not see anything wrong in Hughes poetry being one-sided, if by that he meant concentrating on one particular subject. His capacity to rise to fame should depend on the quality of his poetry and not on his subject matter. In fact, being one-sided should give the poet greater intensity because of proximity to his subject. I believe that what separates any artist from the masters is the quality of his craftsmanship—not the subject. James Baldwin also felt that Hughes used neither his talent nor the rich linguistic culture of the Black race to full advantage. Baldwin felt that Hughes:

> . . . has in his sermons the prayers and power and beat of Negro speech and music. Negro speech is vivid because it is private. It is a kind of emotional shorthand, by means of which Negroes express not only their relationship to each other but their judgment of the White world. Negro language expresses what they are designed to protect, what they are designed to convey. But he has not forced them into the realm of art where their meaning would become clear and overwhelming. (p. 20).

Baldwin, in that piece, was concerned only with the poet's use of language for vivid, poetic effect. He seemed to imply that the use of language is the classic instrument for high poetic quality. Baldwin was seeing only one aspect that creates poetic quality. He forgot the poet's mastery of his craft, his control of poetic texture, his control of the mechanics, his rooted philosophic vision, his commitment to subjects both comic and tragic and his perpetual drive for universal excellence. All these skills create high poetic quality. Hughes may have mastered all forms of Negro speech and dialect, but without mastery of his craft, he would still have been a lousy poet!

In this text I will engage in a critical discussion of whether Hughes was able to dramatize in his poetry the trauma and tragic history of the Negro. My discussion of historical themes will be continued to: *The Negro Speaks of Rivers*, *The South* and *A Daybreak in Alabama*. In discussion of Christian themes, I will concentrate on *At the Feet of Jesus* and *Prayer*. In dealing with the problem of the Mulatto, I will examine *The Cross* and *Mulatto*.

The first poem that deals with Negro history is *The Negro Speaks of Rivers*, which recounts the history of the Negro from his rise in Egypt to his fall in Mississippi and New Orleans.

> I have known rivers.
> I have known rivers ancient as the
> world and older than the flow of
> human blood in human veins.

The key word in the first sentence is "rivers" which can be seen as a metaphor for the history of the Negro, or as a literary river that fills its banks during flood and dries out during drought. If the river is a metaphor for Negro history, then the first sentence becomes an evocation of a patient existence for the Negro who has endured humiliation, hardship and degradation. In the second sentence, the poet emphasizes the notion of longevity. Here the Negro seems to have been the first man on earth. But what did this longevity mean to the Negro? Did it translate into civilization, inventions or overwhelming human achievements? The benefits associated with longevity are revealed in the next stanza where Hughes recounts the gains in civilization and achievements of the Negro from his rise in Egypt where he built pyramids, to his invention of laws at the Euphrates, and finally, to his fall at Mississippi and New Orleans. But in trying to rewrite Negro history, Hughes shows his lack of understanding of African history. The history of the Negro does not start in Egypt and continue through the Congo to the Mississippi. African history starts in the Congo and runs through Egypt. This poem, to be accurate, should have begun Negro life in the Congo, taken it through Egypt and then on to Mississippi. Perhaps this historical error was deliberate. Hughes may have wanted to start the history at its highest point and end at its lowest. This structure of history would fit the fall of the tragic hero. It is important to note that the Negro, because of his achievements in Egypt and Euphrates, assumes in the poem, the power and image of a god—he "looked upon the Nile and raised pyramids". In Egypt, therefore, the Negro did not just blossom in civilization—he even took on the image of sublime deity.

The final stanza reinforces the Negroes stubborn tenacity:

I have known rivers,
Ancient, dusky rivers,
My soul has grown deep like the rivers.

This constant repetition of "I have known rivers" really emphasizes the sense of longevity, patience and tolerance. But there is nothing typically tragic about this poem. There are no tragic situations for the persona, no tragic display even in the language, no extreme excitement in the inventions in Egypt or horror at the fall in Mississippi. The poem, to me, flows like an ordinary history of an ordinary event.

Alain Locke regards the poem as having:

> Primitive fatalism at the back of its nonchalance, the ancient force of its pet colloquialism, the tropic abandon and the irritableness of its sorrow and laughter, the deep tragic undertone pulsing in his verse (p. 26).

Alain Locke certainly exaggerates the quality of this poem. The primitive images in the power are the names of "Egypt," the "Congo River," and the "Euphrates." But there is nothing fatalistic in character and nature, direct or indirect, in the evocation of these ancient names. The tropes certainly exist in the "Congo", "Egypt", "Euphrates", "Soul" and "River". The poem certainly does not carry anything comic or any tragic evocation of these tropes that are irresistible. As for the "deep tragic undertone pulsing" in the veins of this poem, I cannot see it. Alain Locke ascribes to the poem qualities which are not there. For a poem to carry the force that Locke describes, the symbols must evoke excitement and horror, the persona must suffer and exult, the message must have an undertone of subdued horror and enchantment.

However, if *The Negro Speaks of Rivers* recounts the Negro sojourn, *Aunt Sues Stories* is a lyrical, nostalgic song and history. *Aunt Sues* is a history of the Negro in America as seen through the eyes of an old Black woman. *Aunt Sues* is a history as well as a recapitulation of that history. She recounts the suffering of the slaves through their labor in the hot sun, at night and throughout the day. As a song it carries a lyrical nostalgia that emphasizes the "dewy night," the "hot sun" on the slaves at the bank of the river. This sad, beautiful but tragic song weaves through the present serenity and silence, fused with the serenity of the river, with music and song, in an evocation of a sad and dreary history. The life of the Negro thins into the night as a history and emerges from this veiled past into the present, in a beautiful evocation of the past. The poet pours emotions into it, then controls the emotions letting them filter gently through music to the ears of children. This is a good demonstration of a lyric playing with sentiments.

It is my belief that Hughes does not engage in the dramatization of the trauma and the tragic nature of Negro history. Hughes has not:

> . . . brought to bear on literary problems philosophic equipment of comparable authenticity. He does not have the sense of history, the rootedness of imagination in time and place that is solid and acute. (Steiner, p. 42).

To capture the spirit and nature of Negro tragedy, perhaps Hughes should have aspired to write poetry in the same spirit and perfection as the Greek poet, Homer. It is of interest that the critic Schiller marveled at ". . . Homer's impassiveness, at his ability to communicate grief and terror in perfectness of tone" (Steiner, p. 113). In Homer, Steiner claims one sees that:

> The calm of the narrative is nearly inhuman, but in consequence the horror speaks naked and moves us unutterably. Moreover, Homer never sacrifices the steadiness of his visions to the needs of pathos. (p. 114).

A reader of Hughes' poetry cannot find "this impassiveness," this "ability to communicate utmost grief and terror in perfectness of tone." Hughes' poetry sounds like a lyrical recital of old memories of old griefs. Perhaps the lyric is not a proper medium to dramatize the tragic history of a race. The lyric is too playful and sentimental. The critic Croce stated that, "A lyric poet either sings his personal sentiments or narrates the deeds of other men" (p. 629). Hughes recounts only feelings, he does not really dramatize them. Chidi Ikonne may have been correct when he remarked that *Aunt Sues Stories* ". . . is a celebration of oral tradition—that bastion of Black civilization and cultural experience." (p. 157). This is all this poem is—a lyrical celebration of oral tradition.

This celebration of oral tradition leads a reader directly to Hughes' treatment of racism. Racism is depicted by two poems, *The South* and *Daybreak in Alabama*. The story of *The South* is that of stupidity and bestiality towards the Negro. This hostility to the Negro seems ill-conceived because it is the Negro who really loves the South and would have enriched it through cultural diversity and other creative arts. But no! The South is blinded by evil and so cannot see the light behind the darkness. The most dangerous part of the South is in her duplicity and cruelty. The poem opens with:

> The lazy, laughing South
> with blood on its mouth
> The sunny-faced South,
> Beast-strong,
> Idiot brained.

The South can afford to be "lazy" and "laughing" because the Negroes do their dirty jobs. The South has "blood in its mouth," which suggests the lynchings and the unjust hangings. In the next line, the South takes on the image of a strong beast with the brain of an idiot. This strong, stupid beast loves her own children, but willingly kills Negroes, whose bones the beast "scratches from the dead fires' ashes." In the next line, the poem takes on the image of White farmers who torment Negroes in the cotton fields, working them from sunrise, through the moonlight, till dawn. The poem then suddenly breaks from this catalog of evils in the South, and abruptly begins to describe, seemingly as an afterthought, the beautiful scenery of nature in the South:

> The magnolia-scented South.
> Beautiful, like a woman,
> Seductive like the dark-eyed whore,
> Passionate, cruel,
> Honey-lipped, syphilitic—
> That is the South.

In this section of the poem, Hughes, by describing the wickedness of the South, side by side with the beautiful scenery in nature, allows the poem to gain intensity through the powerful force of juxtaposition where the positive and negative images comment and intensify each others' effectiveness through similarity and difference, through presence and absence, through synthesis and antithesis. The poem holds that constant juxtaposition of the beautiful and the ugly. For instance, the South is beautiful like a woman. But this beautiful woman is like the seductive evil-eyed prostitute who would seduce a man and kill in the next breath. The South is "passionate", but also "cruel." The South is "honey-lipped," but also "syphilitic!" There is a clear indication of love and repulsion which gives one a hint of the poet's feelings about the South.

In the next section of the poem, the persona recoils into the self-pity of a man defeated in love:

> And I, who am Black,
> would love her.
> But she spits in my face.
> And I, who am Black,
> would give her many rare gifts.
> But she turns her back on me.

The Negro, having failed in his craving for acceptance in the South, must now migrate North because she is:

> A kinder mistress
> And in her house my children,
> May escape the spell of the South.

As if tired of sad stories, the poem, *Daybreak in Alabama* has a happier mood, reflecting racial harmony and tolerance. The poem opens with:

> When I get to be a composer,
> I'm gonna write some music
> about "Daybreak in Alabama."

This song that he intends to compose will contain the physical beauty of people and nature in Alabama. It will be a song with a lofty tone which will rise from the ground like "swan mist" and fall from the sky like "soft dew." This song will contain "tall trees . . . the smell of red clay after rain . . . long, red necks . . . poppy colored faces . . . big brown arms" and:

> The field daisy eyes of Black and
> White Black White Black people.
> And I'm gonna put White hands
> And Black hands and brown
> And yellow hands,
> And red clay earth hands in it.

In the above lines, there is a clear intention and even desire, reflected in the mixing of colors and neutralizing of racial boundaries, to bring about racial harmony. The poet declared quite happily that in playing and dramatizing his music, he would touch everybody with "kind fingers" like beautiful dew from heaven that touches people in a spring morning. The word "touch" is significant because of the sensitivity of segregation towards human contact between the races.

In the two poems about racism, Hughes showed feelings of both attraction and repulsion for the South. But still, his poetry does not show the bitterness of a man who had a direct experience with racism. His experiences as depicted in his poetry, are not as haunting as that of Jean Toomer in his poem, *Carma*:

> Wind is in the cane. Comes along.
> Can leaves swaying, rusty with
> talk,
> Scratching choruses above
> the geneas squawk,
> Wind is in the cane.

In this poem, the word "cane" has double implications. At one level it may stand for a sugar cane plant in a plantation. At another, it may mean a whip for torture. In the mind of the persona in this poem, the double meanings of the cane are frozen to be seen only as an instrument of torture. In this poem, the wind, mysterious and invisible, compels the tool of torture that comes to a victim who is already saturated with abuse. The pathos in this poem comes from the fact that the persona is so saturated with abuse that rather than run away from pain, he calls for more pain to be inflicted on him. There is that calm impassiveness of repressed anger as the persona watches the "cane leaves swaying," the "rusty talk," and the angry "scratching of choruses above the geneas squawk." These harsh rasping sounds of words like, "rusty talk," "scratching choruses" and "squawk," seem to spark fire like one speaking from hell. There is that calm and haunting call for the wind, like the torture, to keep coming to inflict more pain. This constant call by the victim for more torture gives one a feeling that comes close to the yearning and crying of the Greek Sybil in *I Yearn to Die*. Hughes does not engage a reader with that kind of language which is saturated with anger and menacing in its sensations.

The discussion of racism dealt with the history of the Negro in America. Christian themes also deal with the history of Negro contact with Christianity. Christian themes are found in *At the Feet of Jesus* and *Prayer*. In *At the Feet of Jesus*, the Negro stands pitiably begging for mercy. The Negro, having been trained in patience, does not ask for mercy to flow on him. He asks for it in drips and drops, as if to tantalize his craving for mercy. As far as the Negro is concerned his choices are limited because he can trust neither the White man nor Jesus. He therefore seems completely bound for hell. This view that the Negro is bound for hell is confirmed in the second stanza.

In this stanza, the sinner is asking for forgiveness from *The Little Child Jesus*. The idea of "Little Jesus" has several implications for the Negro Christian. If the Negro is to go to heaven, he must be forgiven his sins by an adult and matured Jesus, who is reasonable, responsible and knows what he is doing. But Little Jesus is a mere child—innocent, naive and possibly irresponsible! It is true that the Baby Jesus has been a savior in common Christian image, but Hughes trivializes the saving power of this little child. That is why the persona asks most mockingly for the little child to reach out his hand and save him. The poet seems to imply

The Other Voice of Harlem Renaissance: Langston Hughes 107

that Christianity is a joke! This skepticism of the Negro towards Christianity comes out clearly in *Prayer*.

The poem opens with three pertinent questions:

I ask you this:
Which way to go?
I ask you this
Which sin to bear?
Which crown to put upon my hair?

The disturbing part of these questions is that they confound answers. Because the Negro cannot with good conscience answer these questions, they heighten his frustration, anxiety and doubt about his humanity, Christianity and existence.

Hughes must be given credit for being able, in this particular poem, to use to his advantage the rich linguistic speech of the Negro. In the poem, there is that constant repetition of questions, the constant insistence, the cadence of speech and the rhythmic pounding, which reflect the speaker's tensions and emotional state. It is a desperate cry from a man on a hot grill who does not know why the pain is being inflicted to begin with.

If the discussion of Christian themes touches on the dilemma of the Negro towards Christianity, the Mulatto theme touches on the dilemma of the Mulatto who is caught between two worlds; rejected first by the White race and then by the Black. The Mulatto theme considers confusion of identity in children born from two racial groups. The poem that dramatizes the confusion and rejection in the Mulatto experience is *The Cross*. In the poem, the Mulatto clings desperately to his White father, while hating his Black mother solely because she is Black and poor. This poem raises issues with Hughes work expressed in *Anonymous Critic* ("Langston Hughes" in *Critical Essays on Langston Hughes*). In that work, the author purports that Hughes was not serious when he claimed that "his soul has grown deep like the rivers."

As a person born and raised in the unified African culture of Nigeria, I cannot understand the Mulatto's animosity for his mother. Does he hate her because she is poor? This poem shows the poet's conscious effort at self-denial and self-negation which is worse than the humiliation of slavery. In *The Cross* the Mulatto clings desperately to his rich White father, but scorns his own mother. This is a story of confusion based on the burden of having to choose to identify with one race. But being neither Black nor White, his choices are closed. He is, therefore, trapped in himself and will fight and fall alone:

> My old man's white old man
> And old mother is black
> If ever I cursed my white old man
> I take my curses back
> If I cursed my black old mother
> And wish she were in hell
> I'm sorry for that evil wish
> And now I wish her well.

This is a classic case of self-hatred, self-negation and confusion which comes with the struggle for racial identity.

The *Mulatto* opens with an emotional announcement, "I am your son white man." This is an emotional plea for acceptance, recognition, pity and the hope of movement into society's mainstream. A rejection will certainly create desperation and humiliation at the end of the line. And the response that the son gets consolidates the fears of the reader: "You are my son like hell!" This rejection is likely to create humiliation, melancholy and despair for the child. But the real tragedy in this poem is that while the Mulatto is rejected by his father, he also rejects his Black brothers. He is, therefore, a born loser. The rejected also rejects! But to repay the Mulatto, the Black race turns around and rejects him. This leaves him lonely, isolated, dejected and decrepit. That is why he has to, "Git back there in the night, you ain't white." The rejection by the Black race completes the cycle of rejection for the Mulatto. The saving grace in this poem is in the joy and beauty in nature. It is amusing that while man is busy discriminating, nature seems to smile at man's shallowness.

It is, therefore, significant that the sky over Georgia is full of "stars," the scent of the pine wood "strings" the air, the "moonlight" is scattered everywhere. The poet seems to mock here a human race which is oblivious to the lessons of peace, harmony, joy and friendship shining out through nature.

A reader looking for answers for Hughes' fame as a Negro poet will find them in Baxter Miller's speculations:

> Of the four major Black American writers—Richard Wright, Ralph Ellison, James Baldwin and Langston Hughes—the latter is probably

most highly regarded and one would wonder why? He gave us no single work which aroused public scorn or sympathy, as did Wright's *Native Son*, nor did he write any masterpiece which rivals Ralph Ellison's *Invisible Man*, in overall unity and structure. Similarly, Hughes left us no literary production which considered alone equals *Invisible Man* in philosophic profundity. Yet who among these other three attempted as much as Hughes? (p. 46).

Hughes' greatness rests on the fact that he tried so much, but succeeded so little.

Bibliography

Anonymous Critic. *Langston Hughes. In Critical Essays on Langston Hughes*. Boston, Mass: G. K. Hall and Co. 1986.
Baldwin, James. *Weary Blues. In Critical Essays on Langston Hughes*. Boston, Mass: G.K. Hall and Co. 1986.
Bass, H.G. *Langston Hughes*. New York: Random House, Inc. Vantage Books. 2nd edition. 1990.
Barthes, Roland. *The Pleasure of the Text*. New York: Hill and Wang, 1975.
Bennet, Gwendolyn B. Ibid. p. 1226.
Berry, Faith. *Langston Hughes. Before and Beyond Harlem*. Westport, Connecticut: 1983.
Bloom, Harold. *Langston Hughes. Modern Critical Views*. New York: Chelsea.
Burke, Kenneth. *A Grammar of Motives*. Berkeley, Los Angeles: University of California Press, 1969.
Croce, Benedetto. *Aesthetics*. Translated by Douglas Ainslie. London, 1929. From the 4th Italian edition. The last Italian edition is the 6th.
Cullen, Countee. *Poet on Poet. Opportunity*. 4th March, 73. 1926.
Donne, John. *Death be Not Proud*. In *The Norton Anthology of English Literature*. New York: W.W. Norton, 1997.
Eliot, T.S. *The Love Song of J. Alfred Prufrock*. In *The Norton Anthology of English Literature*. New York: W.W. Norton, 1997.
Grimke Weld, Angelina. Ibid. p. 943.
Hughes, Langston. Selected Poems. 1st Vintage Classics edition. New York: Vintage Classics, 1959.
Hurston N., Zora. *Their Eyes Were Watching God*. New York: Harper and Collins, 1999.
Johnson Douglas, Georgia. The Norton Anthology of African American Literature. (General Editors) New York: W.W. Norton, 1979.

Keats, John. *When I have Fears that I May Cease To Be*. In *The Norton Anthology of English Literature*, New York: W.W. Norton, 1997.

Knopf, A.A. *Langston Hughes Selected Poems*. 2nd edition. New York: McClelland and Stewart Ltd. 1959.

Lipking, Lawrence. *The Life of the Poet*. From *The Southern Review* 21 #3. July 1985.

Locke, Alain. *Weary Blues*. *Palms*. 20 April 1926-27: 27-28.

Mullen, J. Edward. *Critical Essays on Langston Hughes*. Boston, Mass: G.K. Hall and Co. 1986.

O'Daniel, B.T. Langston Hughes. *Black Genius. A Critical Evaluation*. New York: William and Morrow and Company, Inc. 1971.

Sarte, Jean Paul. What is Literature? Cambridge, Mass: Harvard University Press, 1988.

Spencer, Anne. Ibid. p. 946.

Steiner, George. *A Reader*. New York: Oxford University Press. 1984.

Tracy, C.S. *Langston Hughes and the Blues*. Urbana and Chicago: University of Illinois Press. 1988.

Wordsworth, William. *The Preface to the Literary Ballads*. In *The Norton Anthology of English Literature*. New York: W.W. Norton, 1997.

About the Author

Dr. Egar is currently an Associate Professor of English and the Chairman for the Department of English, Theatre and Mass Communication at the University of Arkansas at Pine Bluff.

He recently published a rhetorical textbook with the title: *The Rhetorical Implications of Chinua Achebe's, Things Fall Apart.* Published by UPA June 2000.

He holds a Ph.D. in English from the University of Texas, Arlington, and another Ph.D. in Higher Education from the University of North Texas in Denton, Texas. He has completed two other books: *African Names in Heaven*, and *The Frosty Silence* (A novel) that are awaiting publication.